Fight Fear
and
Foster Faith

Fight Fear
and
Foster Faith

*Gain the Hope & Courage You Need
to Overcome Difficult Circumstances*

JANA FLAIG

TESTIMONIALS

"*Fight Fear and Foster Faith* is a celebration of survivorship ... a source of comfort and understanding for others who fight this devastating disease. Jana's heart and humor light up every page."
   – **Sandy Stoddard, Community Services Director/California Division/American Cancer Society, Inc.**

"This book is the perfect prescription for lifting spirits, side effects including providing encouragement and hope."
   – **Lee-may Chen, M.D., Gynecologic Oncologist, UCSF Helen Diller Family Comprehensive Cancer Center, San Francisco**

"An excellent balance of bravery, wisdom and humor! This book will be a great encouragement to others going through cancer, and it will help those of us 'outsiders' to have greater understanding and compassion."
   – **Diana L. James, Author of Bounce Back Series, Radio/TV Host**

"More than a survivor, Jana is a thriver. Fight Fear & Foster Faith is a survival guide for you or anyone you know who is afflicted with a life-threatening or debilitating illness."
   – **Sharon Souza, Author of *Unraveled*, and *Every Good & Perfect Gift*, and *Lying on Sunday***

"*Fight Fear and Foster Faith* will give you strength along with the added power of humor, empathy and courage."
   – **Bill Taylor, Radio Personality, KFWB Los Angeles, KMLE Phoenix**

"Heroic, courageous and wonderfully funny!"
   – **Shelly Simas, Director, Lavish Women's Conferences**

Jana Flaig's website can be found at www.JanaFlaig.com

Scripture quotations are from The Holy Bible, New International Version®. Copyright ©1973, 1978, 1984 by International Bible Society. Used by permission of Zondervan, NIV Study Bible (Fully Revised). Copyright © 1985, 1995, 2002 by the Zondervan Corporation. All rights reserved.

Quotations from *The Tongue, A Creative Force*, by Charles Capps. Copyright © 1995, 1976, by Charles Capps, Capps Publishing, England, Arkansas.

Cover photo by Ed Litfin.

Library of Congress Cataloging-in-Publication Data

Flaig, Jana

Fight fear and foster faith: gain the hope & courage you need to overcome difficult circumstances / by Jana Flaig.

ISBN-13: 978-0615723532
ISBN-10: 0615723532

Printed in the United States of America.

for my husband Frank,
who over the years continued to encourage me to put my story in book form. Actually, it was more like nagging … "Write your book!" "Write your book!" "Write your book!"

for our teenaged son Luke,
who had to listen to my comedic stories as I drove him to-and-from school each day. Not once did he attempt to jump out of the car while it was moving. He did, however, groan when I told him, "Someday you'll tell these same stories to your kids as you drive them to school."

in remembrance of my mother,
Andee Flaig Albrecht, who shared my sense of humor and taught me how to find the funny in life.

TABLE OF CONTENTS

FOREWORD

Jana's amazing gift of comedy has set her apart as a cancer survivor. Despite her once frail body, she displayed an iron will to persevere and defeat one of the deadliest forms of cancer. Her unwavering faith and power to laugh, even in the bleakest hours, reveals a strong determined woman who inspires and gives hope to others. I applaud her transparency and wit that carried her through the toughest of times. A must-read. Her story will tickle your soul and warm your heart.

Irene Spencer, NY Times Best Selling Author of
Shattered Dreams: My Life as a Polygamist's Wife

ACKNOWLEDGMENTS

JEAN DANNA, my funny meter, who for years over long distance phone calls listened to and critiqued my comedy material. She also sent unique birthday gifts to me, some of which I use as visuals in this book and props in my speaking presentations.

CAROLE GRAHAM, long-time friend, kept me on God's track by reminding me of the ministry side of this book, not just finding the funny in my fight against cancer. I couldn't have survived those first few days home from the hospital without her help. Her custom-made quilt throw warmed my rented hospital bed and my heart.

SHARON K. SOUZA, author *Unraveled, Every Good & Perfect Gift*, and *Lying on Sunday*, showed me the ropes of getting my book published. What I didn't know about commas could fill a book. And they did. She helped with punctuation too.

DIANA L. JAMES, author Bounce Back Series, speaker, mentor, friend, introduced me to the National Speakers Association, NSA, in 1990. For years we met monthly at Hoff's Hut restaurant to encourage one another as we discussed our books and speaking engagements.

LERA CHAPMAN STILES, dear friend, deceased, who taught me by example how to battle cancer with grace and dignity.

BILL TAYLOR, award-winning radio personality, impressionist, laughed at the stories I told him and said he can't wait to read my book. He said so in one hundred different voices.

EDWARD LITFIN, photographer, who took my professional headshots with wig and bald, cover photo, and other visuals included in this book.

MIKE METCALF, owner/operator/cook of Avenue Grill, who enthusiastically and warmly welcomed the Been There—Got The Wig!® Breakfast Club. He has a heart for people that's bigger than his giant flapjacks, which hang over the edge of a ten-inch dinner plate.

FRANK RUIZ, teacher Jim Elliot Christian High School, who helped me by taking some of the photographs included in this book.

ANDREA McILWAIN, R.N., my wonderful infusion nurse, who took great care of me and watched over me, one chemo session at a time.

DR. KATHRYN BECKMAN, OD, who encouraged me to record the lessons God taught me throughout my long-fought journey to a deeper faith.

DONNA GOLDBERG, inspirational speaker, writer, who by the telling of her story, emboldened me to revisit pain in order to encourage others, and give God the glory for what He has done in my life.

ELIZABETH SYPNIESKI, my friend who bought me the comfy warm-up suit I wore to each chemo session and doctor appointment; and who brought countless bowls of spaghetti and quiches to my door during the months I wasn't able to cook for myself or my family.

DALE EDWARDS, Pastor, and wife SHERRI, who came to the hospitals at 6 A.M. to pray with me before each surgery. They were a great comfort and blessing when I couldn't even pray for myself.

JOANN LEE, friend, Women's Ministry leader, my cheerleader. Thanks for going to chemo with me.

AMY MIRANDA, speaker, who is going to include my name in the acknowledgment page when she writes her book.

KATHI MARTENS, Secretary, Jim Elliot Christian High School, who assisted me in the office with P.A. announcements when I was Principal for a Day.

DAVID COUCHMAN, Administrator, Jim Elliot Christian High School, who trusted me with his position and gave me cart blanche. What was he thinking?

JUDI HARRISON, hair dresser, friend, who walked beside me during those sensitive early days of hair loss due to chemotherapy. Thanks for the buzz job.

BOBBIE STOLLER, Owner, The Wig Palace, thank you for the fabulous custom fitted wigs that were a blessing to me and all the women who wear them.

Dr. JOE ZEITER, Eye Medical Group, who through Lasik eye surgery restored my vision and turned back the clock thirty years. Now I can see the clock on the wall. The post-surgery photo was his idea.

JILL SWANSON, author, speaker, NSA, fashion and color consultant, who periodically chided me in emails, "Jana, write the book!"

Chemo Buddies pictured left to right in the Been There — Got The Wig!® Breakfast Club flyer: RHONDA WASMUNDT, WILMA ZAHOROWSKI, ROSIE CUEVAS WAHLEN, JANA FLAIG.

CAMERON BURGETT, LVN, who brought humor and a positive attitude to my otherwise week-from-hell-in-the-hospital-including-first-major-surgery-eighty-staples-and-ovarian-cancer-life-changing-experience. Thanks for the Fall Risk sign from my hospital room door.

INTRODUCTION

Before cancer, I had no fear because I thought I was in control of what happens to me in life. I even got a T-shirt which asserts that notion:

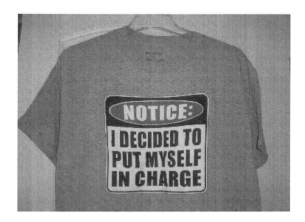

After watching relatives and friends battle cancer, I decided I would not be the one woman out of three to become a cancer patient. I took charge and became a health nut. I subscribed to *Prevention Magazine*, and faithfully followed the cancer prevention tips.

I ate blueberries, I took several anti-cancer supplements daily, I started exercising, including weight lifting. I did so well, I considered training for a body building competition. My goal was to be in the best physical shape I'd ever been in by my next birthday.

During that time, I had all six symptoms of ovarian cancer, but neither my doctors nor I knew that those symptoms fit together to signal the deadliest gynecologic cancer. After months of being misdiagnosed, I finally went into the hospital ER where CT scans revealed a growth on my ovary the size of a grapefruit. The on-call physician recommended I see a gynecologist.

One week later, while performing what she believed would be a routine hysterectomy, my doctor found ovarian cancer which had spread. I was more than afraid. I was stunned and devastated in the same moment. All that money spent on blueberries and anti-cancer supplements. Needless to say, I cancelled my subscription to *Prevention Magazine*.

I knew God did not give me cancer, but He used that trauma in my life to draw me into a closer walk with Him.

Through this life-changing experience, I've learned that when I became a Christian, God did not give me a pass to avoid any hard time or sorrow. What He did do is season that hard time, that sorrow. Like a chef seasons food with spices to temper, soften, improve it, God used His spices (peace, strength, courage, a cheerful heart, faith, comfort, hope) to season my trial.

For some, it may be divorce, job loss, death of a loved one, foreclosure, illness, or other difficult circumstance that brings fear and doubt that undermine faith. My hardship was cancer. I believe God walked me through that valley and gave me the tools I needed to endure every step, to fight fear along the way, foster faith, and gain the hope and courage I needed to be an over-comer.

Chapter One
"OOOH THAT'S THE WORST OPERATION YOU COULD HAVE!"

My mom taught me "never let them see you sweat." In this application it meant no matter how scared I was, or how much pain suffered, I must maintain my composure as I was prepped for my first time as a patient in the hospital. I was determined to be strong and tough it out. That was my resolve.

My resolve lasted five minutes. I could not hold back my tears as the nurse repeatedly jammed an IV needle into the back of my left hand, unsuccessfully trying to find the vein. I finally refused to let her try again, and requested she get someone else. In addition to being scared and in pain, I became cranky and, regrettably, was rude to the staff. There went my candidacy for the favorite patient award.

I desperately needed someone to comfort me, so I felt relieved when one of my neighbors, who I didn't know was a nurse, came around the curtain and said she was assigned to me. Even though I knew her, I was still embarrassed as she helped me get undressed and into a surgical gown. After telling her I was there for a total hysterectomy, I expected her to defuse my fear. But I was wrong.

She winced, shook her head and said, "Oooh, that's the worst operation you could have!" At first I thought she was joking to cheer me up with a little hospital humor. But then she continued, "Hhmmm, that's really bad." I strongly told her to knock it off, I was extremely upset, and I needed to hear only positive words of encouragement. She nodded.

As she wheeled my gurney to the operating room, she sucked in air through her teeth and repeatedly declared my fate, "Painful. Painful.

Painful." By that time the anesthesiologist's happy juice had started to kick in. I had requested the 1960's version. I figured as long as I had to go, it might as well be in a Yellow Submarine, like the animated psychedelic submersible in the Beatles' movie and title song. As I slipped into unconsciousness, I hoped my neighbor-the-nurse was exaggerating, that it wouldn't be as bad as she predicted. It wasn't.

IT WAS WORSE

Following an early morning surgery on Thursday, I expected to wake up in my room that afternoon to find my husband, Frank, at my bedside. Instead, I awoke in the middle of the night two days later, alone in a dark room, in pain, immobilized with tubes and a cast-like bandage that ran the length of my torso. It felt like my entire body was on fire. Minutes passed like hours.

I had questions but no answers. Was it day? Was it night? What time was it? Why wasn't my husband at my bedside waiting for me to wake up? Why did he abandon me? Why hadn't the nurses come to put out the flames? I drew in a labored breath and opened my mouth to call for help, but instead affirmed, "God, I still love you."

I remembered I was in the hospital for a total hysterectomy, but in my sedated state I was confused. I had expected a small bikini line incision and manageable pain; not this huge cut and pain so excruciating and unrelenting that it could not be relieved by the morphine drip.

When a nurse came to check on me, I asked her, "why does it hurt so badly?" She said, "They had to do more surgery than they originally planned." I didn't know what to think of her explanation. But I didn't like the sound of it.

Frank later told me what was supposed to be a routine hysterectomy, taking an hour and a half, turned out to be a three hour procedure. He said when the operation exceeded the hour and a half, he knew something was wrong. And when the doctor finally came out to the waiting room to talk with him, she asked, "Do you want the good news or the bad news?

Frank answered, "I want both." Doctor: "The good news is the operation went well. The bad news is we found cancer."

I didn't wake up during the long hours Frank spent sitting at my bedside until sometime Saturday afternoon. My step-daughter, Julie, was also there, standing next to her dad at the foot of my hospital bed. Before I could ask how the operation went, her face told me the news wasn't good.

Soon the doctor arrived and reported to me she had found ovarian cancer, which had spread. In addition to the large tumor on my left ovary, a second tumor had formed in the pelvic cul-de-sac, and cancer cells were found in the omentum (the fatty apron that covers the stomach and intestines) which was also removed. I was labeled stage 3c.

She said I had "the second largest operation they perform in the hospital today." I was cut from the pelvic bone all the way up to my ribs and had over eighty staples, some of which were crisscrossed or overlapping.

As if that wasn't bad enough, the doctor added that the cancer was hormone receptive, so she took me off estrogen supplements cold turkey. That might explain the feeling of my body on fire when I awoke from surgery. For the first time, I was experiencing full-blown raging hot flashes after seventeen years of staving them off with hormone replacement therapy. I was in a world of hurt, and I could not see beyond my next liquid meal.

The doctor added I was now "officially a Cancer Survivor. Formerly, one had to live five years beyond cancer diagnosis to earn that emblem, but that designation has been broadened to include all cancer patients, from the day cancer was found to the day they die."

I suspected that was her attempt to encourage me before launching into the prognosis. As I listened, the words cancer, chemotherapy, surgeries, each one, hit me like a sock in the nose. My brain was reeling. In those few moments, to my dismay, decades of faith were chipped away and I was down for the count.

Ecclesiastes 9:4 asserts: "Anyone who is among the living has hope — even a live dog is better off than a dead lion!" At that point I felt more kinship with the lion than with the dog. My spirit totally defeated, I silently reached out to God: *Do you know what I'm going through? Lord, are you in this with me?*

Like a whisper, Jeremiah 29:11, came to mind: "I know the plans I have for you declares the Lord, plans to prosper you and not to harm you, plans to give you a hope and a future." In that instant I felt peace pour slowly over me from the top of my head to the tip of my toes. God's Word gave me the reassurance I needed that He knew what I was going through, He was with me and, most importantly, He was in charge of my future. From there I could start to regain hope.

I ADAPTED TO HOSPITAL LIFE

The best thing about my week in the hospital was my new nurse, Cameron, who was professional, efficient, charming and good-looking. He made me want to be a better patient, a SUPER PATIENT.

I was surprised at how quickly he got me up out of bed and walking with a walker. It was only one day after I awoke from surgery. I remember how weak and light-headed I was; and yet driven to impress him with my overachiever's imagined post-surgery athletic ability. I held onto the walker with both hands, and slowly took baby steps from my bed by the window all the way to the restroom and back. To my chagrin, it was totally exhausting. I had to stop repeatedly and rest along the way; and almost couldn't make it back to my bed without his assistance. I was humbled. So much for showing off.

While I was up, I noticed a "NO FALL ZONE" sign posted on the door of my hospital room. I wasn't sure if that sign was displayed as an encouragement to me, a warning, or an edict.

My nurse laughed when I told him I wanted that sign to use as a prop in a speech presentation. I added that it was my intention to take it anyway, but I would rather he give it to me as a souvenir when I checked out of the hospital. He took the sign off the door and gave it to me on the spot. That made me happy, but then I wondered *if no sign on the door meant I was no longer in the NO FALL ZONE.*

By the fifth day, I was required to push myself further by walking up and down the hospital hallway. As he walked next to me, my nurse told me to tell him if I felt dizzy or faint along the way.

In other words, it was important I identify myself as a fall risk. He gave me this different hospital sign.

I chose to wear this warning placard taped to the front of my hospital gown as I strolled the hallways. After all, this notice wouldn't do me any good left behind, affixed to my hospital room door.

I'll never see this guy again. Once I'm out of this hospital, odds are against me running into him around town. And besides, he has so many patients coming in and out of the hospital, he won't remember me. That's what I told myself in order to reduce the embarrassment I felt as my cute, charming nurse dressed my incision before releasing me.

I tried to chalk up the experience to just another awkward moment in the life of a patient. Throughout my week-long hospital stay, I gained firsthand knowledge of what people mean when they say "there's no modesty in hospitals."

Per hospital regulations, upon my release an aide pushed me in a wheelchair from my room on the third floor down to the curb. Frank had walked ahead to get the minivan and pull up to the entrance. The toughest part of the drive home was getting myself in and out of the van without being able to twist or bend, due to the eighty staples and heavy bandages covering my body from the crotch to the breast bone.

FIRST CANCER, NOW THIS

A few months later, I took some cookies to welcome a new family on the block. I knocked on the door and, boy, was I shocked when it opened and there stood my cute, favorite nurse. He greeted me with his big charming smile, which told me yes, indeed, he remembered me. I could feel my face turn red.

I met his family, gave them the cookies, and quickly got out of there. As I hurried down the street to my home, all I could think about was, *Oh shoot! Now there are two neighbors on my block who have seen me naked!*

TIP # 1:

Never let them see you sweat. Being courageous doesn't mean we have no fear. Courage is persevering in spite of fear.

TIP #2:

Request the 1960's version of the anesthesiologist's happy juice if you're ever in the hospital for major surgery.

Chapter Two

The TWILIGHT ZONE

That first operation and long recovery was a shock to me and my family; but being told I had cancer was a bigger blow, like being ushered into The Twilight Zone, an intangible place, where strange or macabre circumstances occur, as depicted in the   television series which combined drama, science fiction, suspense, horror, and ended each story with an unexpected twist. I imagined hearing the creator and narrator, Rod Serling, as he opened each episode: *"There's a signpost up ahead ... you've just entered the Twilight Zone."*

While the doctor stood by my hospital bed and recounted that she had found ovarian cancer, I envisioned the word CANCER hanging in the air over my head like a cloud. After she added I'll face months of chemotherapy and the possibility of multiple surgeries down the line, my brain shut down, and I didn't hear another word the doctor said.

As I sat frozen in my chair, it took all the strength I had to keep a calm and controlled expression on my face. The internal mantra, *Never let them see you sweat*, was my focus. I didn't want anyone in the room to know, Jana had already left the building, mentally and emotionally.

Although cancer was not a surprise to God, I was totally blown away! I've never felt so utterly alone. I've never needed God more.

That was a life-changing moment, a surreal experience, like being stamped on my forehead with an expiration date. And that date, according to the doctors, could be shorter than the shelf life of a Hostess Twinkie.

My worst fear had come true. I was baffled as to how this could happen when I did everything commonly known to avoid The BIG C; and as a backup, I periodically thanked God that I did not have cancer.

My mind spun in an alternate reality, a bizarre world where everything is unexpected and unbelievable. The idea of God letting me die too soon was unfathomable. When I was finally able to form a thought in response to the C word, I was surprised it wasn't of fear, but of fashion, as I heard myself say: "I'd better start wearing my good clothes everyday."

DENIAL KICKED IN

An internal monologue argued my case: *It just can't be. There has to be some mistake. Maybe the files were mixed up. That could have happened. Or maybe they could switch my file with someone who's depressed and wants to die. I couldn't possibly be that one woman out of three to get cancer because I was a health nut. It can't be my turn. This is the best time of my life. Our son still has a few years before going off to college, my husband of thirty years survived prostate cancer, our beloved family dog is still alive; and we recently moved from bustling Southern California to a small peaceful town in the wine country of Northern California, where we live in our dream house. It must be a mistake.*

My life was going good. And when life is good, it's like a Christmas

stocking filled with wonderful gifts. The shock of cancer felt as if someone put a four-ton elephant of fear into my stocking.

I was instantly terrified that I would not live the long life with my family that I expected. Our son was only in junior high and I want to see him grown up, graduated from college, established in his field and married with children.

And besides, I have to be around to pick out his wife. He thinks I'm kidding about that.

I was not only afraid my life with my family would end too soon, but it would end before I could fully utilize decades of preparation, training and experience in fulfilling God's purpose for my life. Some of the visions the Lord gave me as a young woman have since come true, but there remain other visions which are yet to be fulfilled. I'm not done yet.

BUCKET LIST

There were many things I still needed to do or wanted to accomplish that I hadn't gotten around to. For example, have my eyesight improved with Laser Vision Correction so I'd no longer be dependent upon trifocals; create my own website including video and audio clips; be Principal-for-a-Day at a Christian high school; learn how to be more spontaneous; expand my ability to embrace life.

I also considered getting a tattoo. And I wanted to live long enough to regret having gotten a tattoo. I scrubbed the idea when I realized that such a regret would overcome me in about twenty minutes.

That was not the first time in my life I toyed with the notion of getting a tattoo. In college, 1968, I wanted to get a daisy tattoo on my big toe but my mother would have killed me, so I chickened out. Now that she's passed on, and I'm the parent, I could do whatever I wanted.

If I were to get a tattoo, I may still prefer a small, tasteful, cute daisy no bigger than the size of a quarter, not the large body-covering designs many people wear today. Even then, I'd ink a spot on my body that I could cover up.

In 2009, I came close to fulfilling my youthful fantasy by going into the "Get It and Regret It" tattoo parlor with my girlfriend, Tricia. I held her hand and reminded her to b-r-e-a-t-h-e while she was tattooed; and I took pictures of the inking process for her scrapbook.

I left the parlor tattoo-less, not due to fear of the needle, but due to indecision. I just could not choose that one design I would wear for the rest of my life. I also suspected the "Regret It" half of the establishment's moniker was routed in truth, so I leaned toward declining the artwork.

The final determinant was what the big, burly, tattoo artist said. "I'll tell you the same thing I told my own mother. Even after you are dead and buried and your body turns to dust in the grave, that tattoo will still be there." Enough said. No tattoo for me.

TIP #3:

Wear your good clothes everyday. Don't save them for a special occasion, or for someday when you'll be well again or life returns to normal.

When you look better, you feel better. When you feel better, it's easier to have hope.

TIP #4:

Rethink the tattoo idea. I'm just saying.

Chapter Three

ONE MONTH IN A RENTED HOSPITAL BED

The seven days spent in the hospital were just the beginning of my long recuperation. I was not only suffering side effects of major surgery, but extreme weakness caused by anemia and subsequent weight loss, from 128 pounds down to 110 pounds, while cancer cells grew undetected inside me for months.

I was eager to go home and get on with the healing process. Several adjustments had to be made, starting with where and how I would sleep.

Those eighty staples which ran the length of my torso prevented any bending movement up and down or turning side to side, so getting into and out of a chair or bed was slow, painful, and nearly impossible unassisted. Climbing the stairs to my second floor bedroom and sleeping in my own flat bed was out of the question.

Solution: we rented an adjustable hospital bed which allowed me to recline with my head and feet elevated. The extended height of the large frame made it easier for me to transition from standing to sitting to lying. This temporary bed was set up in the middle of the family great room, and positioned about four feet in front of the television.

Next to one side of the bed was a TV tray on which I placed my reading glasses, TV remote control, water, phone, etc. On the other side of the bed was a walker, which I needed to pull myself up to standing position and slowly shuffle to the nearby downstairs bathroom or to the kitchen table. That was my reality day after day, week after week, for the next month.

Beyond cancer, I think my husband and son were in shock over the abrupt change in our family's life style during that time. They were accustomed to me buying groceries and household supplies, cleaning, cooking, basically micro managing (but in a good way) everyone's routine. Suddenly I was relegated to full-time cancer patient.

In a plaintive voice my 13-year-old son asked, "You mean for my entire seventh grade you won't cook, or drive me to school, or come to my softball games or do anything?" I didn't have the heart to tell him I was fighting for my life. Nor did I have the courage to advise him that his dad—a man who can't even put the lid back on the peanut butter jar—would be in charge of meals for the two of them for an indefinite period.

I probably would have joined him in his despair if it weren't for the pain meds I was taking, which made me spacey and even knocked me out for a few hours at a time. That I liked. It gave me a short vacation from the nightmare I was living.

Each of us was trying to cope with our own sense of loss. We all needed help.

THE CAVALRY ARRIVES

 Fortunately, my long-time girl-friend, Carole, is a nurse. And bless her heart, she flew down from her home in the Northwest to care for me, and establish a post-surgery routine in my first four days at home. She instructed Frank and me on the proper way for me to get in and out of the rented

hospital bed, and walk to and from the bathroom.

Carole also made sure the refrigerator was stocked with food I could eat, Jell-O, fruit, pudding, eggs, deli-sliced turkey. She also set me up with a schedule for food and taking the medications on time. She thought of everything.

And I was comforted by a beautiful custom-made quilt throw she designed especially for me, which included large red hearts on cobalt blue and burgundy backgrounds. Carole is also an expert quilter (cavernjo.com). Instead of giving me a bell to ring to summon help, Carole gave me a battery operated Mini Bull Horn with siren. In case my family was upstairs and couldn't hear me, I'd just push the little red button and the siren would sound. I tested it once...they thought it was the house alarm, ran down the stairs and out the front door, leaving me behind. It was a good idea, but maybe it would work better with another family.

Carole taught me how to slowly climb the stairs by grasping the banister with both hands and using my legs to lift. It was exhausting and painful. I was surprised how much we use our core for every step. My core was temporarily dead weight, which ached with the slightest movement. Out of strength and out of breath, I had to repeatedly stop to rest.

I hadn't bathed since the morning of my surgery, ten days prior. I knew Carole's nursing experience was my best shot at getting in and out of the shower as safely as possible. She watched me through the shower glass as I sat in a plastic chair and attempted to wash away a week and a half of misery.

The next day it was time for my friend to return home, and for me to go back to my doctor, who would start removing the eighty overlapping surgical staples. The process of ripping the staples out of my flesh, which had healed/bonded around the metal pieces, was so painful I could only stand to have a few removed in one visit.

I was horrified when the doctor simply started to forcefully p-u-l-l out the staples. No shot to numb the area, no Valium, no offer of a blindfold. In between my screams I grabbed her hand and asked, "Don't you have a topical for that?" The answer was a firm "No." I wondered if she had quarreled with her husband earlier in the day.

The doctor did apologize for my pain, but said it was unavoidable. Regardless, I had passed my pain threshold for the day, and after having only a few staples removed, I left the office in tears. Later Frank suggested maybe the doctor wasn't as gentle as I would have liked because she's accustomed to working on patients when they are anesthetized, lying unconscious on the operating table.

I was dreading the removal of more staples. So when I returned to the doctor's office a few days later to try again, I insisted the nurse do the job instead of the doctor.

This time the mood was different, lighter, right from the start. After the nurse called me and Frank to follow her into an exam room, she skipped ahead of us as she joyfully announced, "I just had a piece of chocolate cake."

The first thing she did was apply some topical numbing medicine to the stapled tissue. She had topical! I wondered, *was this her private stash? Why didn't the doctor know about this miracle numbing balm?* I asked this wonderful nurse if she would please give some to the doctor across the hall.

Then, instead of pulling out the staples and ripping flesh, the nurse gently raised one side of the staple, then the other, back and forth until she could easily remove it without making a new tear. It was still a painful process, but bearable. She was able to remove half of the eighty staples, and instructed me to come back again in a few days to take out the rest.

Getting the surgical staples removed was a milestone in my recuperation journey. Once I was free of all that crisscrossed metal, I was better able to bend and move, and with less pain. To complete this dreaded task it only took three office visits, one change of personnel, and one piece of chocolate cake.

TIP#5:

<u>Plan ahead</u>. Teach your family members how to cook for themselves in case you're ever laid up and can't do it. Or at lease show them, again, how to put the lid back onto the peanut butter jar.

Chapter Four
HOW I GOT HERE

As I lay in the rented hospital bed, I reflected upon my medical odyssey which rendered me virtually helpless and facing an uncertain future. Looking back, the first indication that something wasn't right was the overwhelming fatigue which sent me to the couch by 3 p.m. each day. Not at all my usual Type A behavior.

One day in March—nine months before my cancer diagnosis—I picked up my son from junior high. I told him we could not go to the video store as planned because I was so tired I had to go right home and rest. To my surprise he said, "Mom, you've been tired for a year." I realized he was right, it had been months since I could go all day, working and running errands. Being pooped out on the couch by the afternoon was my new norm.

NOT MYSELF

In May 2006, I went to the ob-gyn for my annual exam. I told her I was tired all the time, bloated, gaining weight although I was exercising, eating right and taking Phentermine (appetite suppressant); and for the first time in my life, I was getting up once or twice in the middle of the night to pee. She said I was fine, in menopause, and she upped my prescription dosage for Premarin (estrogen) and Provera (progesterone) to ease my distress.

I told Frank I felt like I was "living in someone else's body." I just did not feel like myself.

By June, constipation was added to my list of symptoms. When I was able to go to the bathroom, I never felt fully relieved. So I went back to my ob-gyn and told her I thought I had a bowel obstruction. She examined me, didn't find anything unusual, and again said I was in menopause and "exhibiting symptoms common to middle aged women." I went home.

The good news was she didn't find anything wrong with me. The bad news was she didn't find anything wrong with me. And I still felt lousy. Echoing in my head was an insistent voice, *They haven't found it yet. Go back to the doctor.*

As summer progressed, so did my discomfort. Now I was experiencing constant pressure, sometimes pain, in the abdomen. Once as I was walking down the stairs at home, I suddenly and violently doubled over in response to a sharp knife-like shooting pain in my mid section. That I knew was not normal.

In late August, I switched to my family general practitioner, and initially got the same "you're a middle aged women" tag. However, in response to my report of nightly multiple peeing episodes, he suspected an uncommonly long-lasting bladder infection for which he tested me. Because my white count was slightly elevated, he believed his diagnosis was correct. He gave me antibiotics and sent me home.

All my symptoms worsened, I continued to weaken, and anemia was added to the list. I knew then it wasn't a bladder infection, because I've had them before. When treated with antibiotics they usually last only a few days, not several months. I made weekly trips to my G.P. throughout September. I believe we both grew more frustrated as we brainstormed to find a cause.

I described an internal pressure, like squeezing. I said repeatedly, "There's something pressing in there." He said he thought I had pulled a muscle while working out in the gym. That's when he gave me a cortisone shot, with an eight inch needle, right into my abdomen. I passed out.

The G.P. said he dismissed the possibility of female cancers because my regular annual pap exam, which I'd had in May, was normal. He did not know, nor did I, there is no screening test for ovarian cancer, and it is not detected in a routine pelvic exam. However, there is the CA125 blood test tumor marker for ovarian cancer, which he had ordered but was not included in my regular blood work results.

Test reordered, more blood drawn, and the CA125 number was 71, clearly exceeding the normal cut off limit of 35. Although I had all six symptoms of ovarian cancer—fatigue, bloating, frequent urination, weight gain, constipation, abdominal pain—and an elevated CA125, neither my doctors nor I knew those symptoms fit together to signal the deadliest gynecologic cancer.

THE SQUEAKY WHEEL

By October, my girlfriend or my husband took me doubled over in pain four times to the doctor's office without an appointment. I told the G.P., "You are seeing me now without an appointment because you haven't found it yet." At each of these visits, I repeatedly asked the doctor if I needed an ultrasound so we could see what was pressing inside, causing such pain, and making me weaker by the day. Each time the response was, "I don't think you need it," or thoughtful silence. He was the doctor.

But I knew my body, and I knew these were not just menopausal symptoms. I insisted something was growing inside me; and I believed all I needed my doctor to do was order an ultrasound so we could find the source, give it a name, and get on with the cure. At that point I felt I wasn't being heard.

November was spent curled up on the couch with a heating pad on my abdomen. It hurt like menstrual cramps, and the heat offered some relief. By that time the anemia had robbed my appetite, and I was too weak to keep going back to doctors who had no answers.

I was misdiagnosed and miserable.

It was the Sunday night after Thanksgiving, and as I laid down on my bed, my body started to shake and literally bounced up and down on the mattress. I could not control it nor stop it. It was terrifying. It took all of my strength to call out to my son and husband who were in other rooms watching TV.

Frank scooped me up in his arms and drove to the emergency room. Within minutes I was prepped for a CT scan. The hospital CT machine was down for repairs, so I was taken on a gurney outside, through the parking lot, in the rain, to a temporary portable scanner housed in a huge trailer. The night was dark and wet and cold and scary.

The on-call doctor gave us the results. "Well, your liver, kidneys, lungs, everything looks perfect, except you have a growth the size of a grapefruit on your ovary." My head was filled with a resounding *DUH!* ... *that's what I'd been telling everyone for seven months, but no one heard me.*

The E.R. doctor ordered the trans-vaginal ultrasound for the next day. That procedure afforded even more detailed pictures of the cause of my problem. By the afternoon I was seen by a different ob-gyn physician who did a physical exam and, in two seconds, felt the tumor and exclaimed, "Oh yeah, there it is, and it's got to come out." She scheduled a total hysterectomy for the following week.

In our pre-op meeting with the ob-gyn doctor, she told Frank and me that she was "90% sure it's not cancer, because when I see cancer, the CA125 is usually 3,000-4,000, not 71." In retrospect, the confidence I felt going into surgery turned out to be false hope. Although the pre-surgery call missed the mark, to her credit, my surgeon did an excellent job removing the cancer once it was discovered. I believe God used her skills to save my life.

THE UPSHOT

For seven months I had been misdiagnosed by two doctors whom I liked and respected. They were not cancer specialists trained in what to look for, so it was with displaced anger that I blamed them for missing it. However, I do rebuke them for not recognizing, or admitting, the answer was beyond their expertise; and for their failure to refer me to a specialist.

That's how I came to spend a month in a rented hospital bed in my family room.

TIP #6:

Go to a specialist at one of the top teaching medical centers when faced with a serious health problem. In Northern California such medical centers include UC San Francisco, UC Davis, or Stanford University.

TIP #7:

Be the squeaky wheel, whether the circumstance is career pursuits, health issues, relationships, etc.

Chapter Five
POSTCARD FROM GOD

I never asked God, "Why me?" However, I considered, *it would have been nice if He had sent me a postcard to forewarn me of my upcoming battle, reassure me of its outcome, and confirm that the test of my faith would result in a closer relationship with Him.* Maybe then I wouldn't have been so afraid along the way. I imagined the postcard would look like this:

And that it would read: "My dear, wonderful, precious, special, favorite daughter Jana" — it's my imagined postcard from God, so it can say whatever I want on it — "just a line to let you know you will soon be stricken with ovarian cancer, fear for your life, endure the pain of major surgery and suffer the ill effects of chemotherapy. But fear not, for I am with you, do not be dismayed for I am your God. I will strengthen you and help you. I will uphold you in my righteous right hand." Signed, God. "P.S.: Don't stock up on hair spray."

In a way, God did send that postcard. I believe He was that unrelenting voice inside me: *Go back to the doctors, they haven't found it yet, go back to the doctors.* Again and again I went back, driven by His perceived voice nudging me to be my own patient advocate.

FOREWARNED IS FOREARMED

God also whispered His assurance by calling to my memory why, years ago, I chose  the Italian charms—Trust, Hope, Jesus the Healer—for the bracelets I've worn almost everyday since. I chose them because I heard Him say, "You'll need these reminders someday." I didn't want to imagine what future hardship I might experience that would necessitate such remembrances. Still, I attached them to my bracelet and, for a moment, I hoped I heard wrong.

I also bought custom-made scripture charms: "No weapon formed against you shall prosper." "Trouble will not come a second time" (This sickness shall leave and not come back again). "I know the plans I have for you declares the Lord, plans to prosper you and not to harm you, plans to give you a hope and a future." That was the biggie.

I learned no matter what I face in life, God is the giver of hope, and He walks with me through the hard time, the sorrow, because He loves me.

Almighty God also gave me a sense of urgency to prepare for Christmas weeks in advance, accompanied by the vexing thought: *You'll be in the hospital by Christmas.* Well, that was a crazy idea because I was the health nut who was never going to be the patient. Regardless, I followed through by decorating the house before November, much earlier than usual, complete with wrapped presents under the tree.

In December, I was a patient in the hospital for the first time in my life. After surgery I went home to a rented hospital bed which was surrounded by Christmas decorations.

ONE FOR THE BOOKS

That's the Christmas I'll never forget. Not only because God forewarned me of the coming trauma and told me to prepare for Christmas early, but because of how He walked me through it with the support of other Christian believers. Sometimes God's love comes in a bowl of spaghetti, a simple gift, or a note from a friend.

My girlfriend, Amy, went public with her note when she submitted an entry to the News-Sentinel contest in which people nominate seniors who have touched their lives in a special way. The Outstanding Seniors chosen were spotlighted in the newspaper. Her entry won, and was featured in the December issue.

Title: JANA IS MY HERO
Description: San Joaquin County's Shining Silver Senior Contest by Amy Miranda for Jana Flaig

SOME GIFTS CAME WITH INSTRUCTIONS

Amy also brought me a new pair of cozy

slippers. And, just in case I was too high from the pain killers, on the bottom of each slipper she wrote the foot on which I should wear it. She didn't really need to go that far. All she had to do was write it on one slipper, and I would have gotten it.

Other gifts came with instructions from the manufacturer, including a list of safety warnings. This warning for the Black & Decker Food Processor: "Do not operate this food processor in the presence of explosives." So if I were dynamiting my kitchen, I should eat out that night.

Or this caution for the Shark Cordless Sweeper: "Do not suck up anything that is burning." Of the numerous warnings in the instruction booklet, that was only number twelve on the list!

And a handy Nose Hair Trimmer with a light which turns on with the unit exclaims a threefold warning:

1. "Avoid looking directly into the light."

2. "Always wear safety goggles while operating trimmer." (Goggles sold separately)

3. "This product is designed for home use only."

One of my favorite little gifts was a big clip which I used to attach my water bottle to the hospital bed rail.

It reminded me of the kind of useful gadget my mother used to put in my Christmas stocking. Part of the fun we had was trying to guess how the device was to be used. Oftentimes, the alternative applications we came up with trumped the original intent.

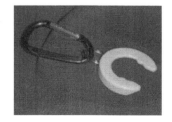

I got a stocking from her each Christmas until I was fifty years old. Beyond that time, even up into her eighties, she still made a stocking for me every year. Unfortunately, she forgot where she hid them.

A PRACTICAL GIFT

My husband, Frank, gave me a gift that was unwrapped. I asked him, "I know this is an unusual Christmas for us with me stuck in this hospital bed, but why didn't you bother to wrap it?"

He said, "It's biblical."

"What do you mean it's biblical?"

He told me, "The three Wise Men brought unwrapped gifts to Jesus."

"How do you know that?"

He said, "Because if the gifts were wrapped, it would say in the Bible, 'after Mary opened the gifts to their son Jesus, she said to Joseph, saveth the paper'."

My husband knew the pain sometimes woke me in the middle of the night, so I kept a book on the hospital bed I could easily pick up and read until I could fall back to sleep. Hence he gave me a very helpful and practical gift ...

... A combination bite guard and reading light.

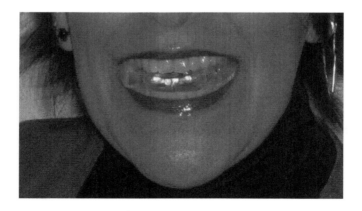

At a point when I didn't even have the strength to pray for myself, let alone get up and do household chores, family and friends carried me through. Their prayers, cards, gifts, and meals were not only help in difficult circumstances, but a manifestation of God's love. "There is no fear in love. But perfect love drives out fear"(1 John 4:18). Through their tireless support, that huge four-ton elephant of fear cancer put in my stocking was cut down to the size of a Beany Baby.

THE "IT" GIFT

Every Christmas there seems to be that one gift you see everywhere. That year it was the Snuggie, the "blanket that has sleeves!" I used to make fun of the people who bought these, until I tried one. To my surprise, it was really warm and soft and cozy. It felt great! And, one-size-fits-all.

I liked sitting on the couch or the rented hospital bed, wrapped in my Snuggie. I was comfortable and comforted, as I slowly regained strength. At times, during the long weeks of recuperation, it seemed as though my world had been reduced to this blanket in which I wrapped myself. And when I had the strength to go out and make a brief trip to the grocery store, it was hard for me to leave this comfort behind.

So I didn't. I just dressed it up by adding a belt. And no one could tell I was wearing my blanket.

Fashion tip #5: Accessorize

I liked the Snuggie so much, I even bought one for my dog.

I would wrap him in his Snuggie like a cocoon. He really liked that. And sometimes, when I just couldn't resist, I threw my slipper across the room and yelled, "Go get it!"

MULTI-FUNCTIONAL

When I get a Christmas gift I really like, I try to get the most out of it by coming up with alternative uses.

For example:

I also used my Snuggie as a handy BBQ cover.

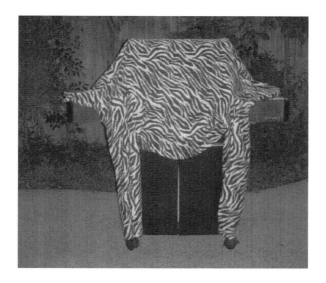

And a cool car cover.

THE BEST GIFT

I asked for the best gift and I received it when I was twenty-four years old, and it's still just the right size to fit into my heart. It's God's gift of His Son Jesus Christ, who was crucified and died for my sins; who was resurrected, and continues to live in my heart as Savior and Lord.

He comes with an extended warranty for eternity. Jesus is the only gift that truly is one size fits all. And all I had to do to receive God's gift was to ask, open my heart, and receive it.

CHEERFUL RECEIVER

The family's traditional holiday decorations, which surrounded me as I lay captive in the rented hospital bed, not only represented our normal Christmas, but reminded me of treasured Christmases past with my mom.

She had a unique way of receiving and opening a gift. As she uncovered the contents she raised her eyebrows, slightly tilted her head and melodically said "OOOOH." We could anticipate this overtly positive response, which she believed disguised whether or not she liked the present.

As an inside family joke, we would sometimes give her a second gift we knew she wouldn't like; then we sat back and waited for her faked response of surprise and delight.

TIP #8:

Ask for help. Afford people the opportunity to be blessed by giving to you. That may include meals, household chores, praying together, encouraging cards, phone calls or visits.

TIP #9:

Say "Yes" if a friend who's visiting asks "Do you want me to vacuum the carpet or wash the dishes in the sink before I leave?"

TIP #10:

Look for the postcards from God in your life. Do not return to sender unread.

Chapter Six
THE SECOND & THIRD OPINION

I wore a protective face mask and hung onto Frank's arm as we slowly walked down the gangway and boarded the Southwest plane to Los Angeles. It was the last thing I expected to be doing only thirty days after major surgery, and just days before I was scheduled to start chemotherapy. The date was pushed back to allow for our trip, despite my oncologist's warning that cancer cells multiply with each passing day. Given the importance of our journey, he reconsidered and added, one week will not make the difference between life or death.

I hoped no one would sit in the open seat next to me, because in my weakened state I was susceptible to catch a bug from another passenger. I could not afford to delay the start of chemo beyond the next week due to illness.

Some of the travelers made brief eye contact, saw my face mask and the small pillow I clutched to my abdomen, then glanced away and walked on. One by one, people walked past my row and took another seat nearer the back of the plane. Maybe the moaning was a slight deterrent too, but I couldn't be sure.

Now that we knew my affliction had a name, ovarian cancer, we chose to travel to the top experts in the Gynecologic Oncology field to get a second and third opinion regarding my upcoming treatment. Frank and I had learned by watching close friends battle various types of cancer, and through his prostate cancer experience, there could be an appreciable difference in the quality of treatment and survival rate depending upon where we went.

Teaching hospitals on the cutting edge of research and application may offer advanced—new & improved—treatment options. For example, the so-called designer drugs, a cocktail or combination of drugs specifically developed to produce certain desired effects in the individual cancer patient.

We were on a mission to save my life, so we booked back-to-back appointments at the Hoag Cancer Center, Newport Beach, and the Cedars-Sinai Medical Center Cancer Institute in Los Angeles, to meet with two of the top doctors in the country specializing in the treatment for ovarian cancer.

We consulted with the heads of the Gynecologic Oncology departments at each hospital. I told each doctor that we had an appointment with the other doctor on the same day, and I asked them both the same questions. They each reviewed my surgical records, performed a pelvic exam, and answered my long list of questions such as, "Which chemo drugs would you use to treat me?" "What's the regimen, how often would I be infused, and for how long at each session?"

Both experts advised me that in the case of ovarian cancer, "No matter where you are in the world, it is the same two drugs—a Platinum compound (Carboplatin) and Paclitaxel (Taxol), given intravenously every three weeks for six treatments." This meant that I could remain in my hometown in Northern California, and still receive the best chemotherapy treatment for my type of cancer.

I was grateful for the opportunity to have my surgical report reviewed by these experts and to ask them, "Would you have done anything differently if you had performed my total hysterectomy, which resulted in the discovery of ovarian cancer?" I realized this was a little like closing the barn door after the horses had run out, but I needed to know.

Both doctors noted my surgeon did not remove lymph nodes, but only visually checked them for the presence of cancer cells. The gynecologic oncologists agreed, they would have gone beyond just visually checking the lymph nodes by removing them for biopsy. They said, "Even if the nodes look clean, there's a thirty percent chance they contain microscopic cancer cells which may metastasize later." I was also advised that my surgeon did nothing wrong by not taking out the nodes, that there are two schools of thought as to whether or not the nodes are automatically removed.

WE NEEDED ADVICE

The doctors didn't tell us what we should do, they just gave us the medical facts and stated our options. Without specific direction our decision-making process was difficult. I tried to elicit a more specific recommendation by making the inquiry personal.

This tactic worked for my husband years ago when he was diagnosed with prostate cancer and given only a thirty percent chance to live three years. He asked his doctor at another unnamed hospital where would he go for treatment. The doctor replied, "Well, if it were me, I wouldn't come here. I'd go to such and such hospital." Frank followed the doctor's candid advice and went to a prostate cancer specialist for treatment. Today he is an eleven year cancer survivor who gives God the glory.

In a blatant effort to get guidance, I asked each oncologist this final question: "If I were your wife and we had a 13-year-old son," or "If you were me and you had a 13-year-old son, what would you do now?" They both stood on their diagnosis and treatment plan.

Perhaps the most important information I gleaned from my time with the gynecologic oncologist in Newport Beach was his answer to the question I didn't have the courage to ask. As he was leaving the exam room, he suddenly stopped, turned around to look me in the eye and asserted, "You didn't cause this. Nothing you did caused ovarian cancer." I hadn't realized until that moment what a burden of blame I had been carrying. I cried tears of relief.

A QUEST FOR MORE FACTS

In addition to my consultation with the ovarian cancer doctor at Cedars-Sinai Medical Center in Los Angeles, we had scheduled a PETT scan P(ositron) E(mission) T(ransaxial) T(omography), which, unlike CT scans, goes beyond revealing images of the soft tissues of the body to signal the presence of cancer. The radiologist told me, "If cancer is there, the PETT scan will light up like a Christmas tree."

My oncologist did not order the PETT scan because he did not believe I needed it; but we wanted the scan in order to gather as much information as possible to arm ourselves for the upcoming fight for my life. The breach in our opinions was mended, and I received the PETT Scan by paying cash for the images. I would receive the results after returning home.

We rushed to return our rental car and make our flight back to Sacramento that night. It had been a long, stressful, emotional day for us both. For me, it was also a personal record—two pelvic exams by two doctors, at two hospitals, in two different counties, all in the same day. The discomfort and embarrassment I felt fueled the tension of the day, and reinforced how much I hated being the patient.

At least we received some more definitive information regarding my situation. A much better help than the four hours we initially spent on the internet when we learned I had ovarian cancer. That was a mistake. With each click of the mouse my computer screen delivered page after page of hopeless statistics about the disease. All the reports announced the same outcome: YOU ARE GOING TO DIE, SOON. The result was total defeat, devastation, hopelessness. I hate technology.

TIP #11:

Get at least a second opinion and get it from a specialist in the field.

Chapter Seven
PLAYING THE CANCER CARD

Soon I noticed people reacted differently to me once they learned I had cancer. One lady came up to me in church and apologized. She said, "I'm sorry I didn't get to know you," and turned and walked away. She just missed her second chance. Another woman approached me and exclaimed, "I'm sooo glad I'm not you!" My friend's mother talked to me on the phone and offered, "The good thing about knowing you are going to die soon is you can write your will."

I received other inane and insensitive comments, such as, "You don't look sick." "You better make out your bucket list." "What does it feel like knowing you're going to die soon?" "How long do the doctors say you have?" They might as well have asked, "Has your husband started dating?"

The most annoying offering I received came from other Christian believers: "Well if you die, you win either way." No! Baloney!! To die twenty-five-plus years too soon, and take me away from my family, was absolutely not a win-win scenario. Sure, I want to go to heaven someday and live forever with Jesus, but not yet.

Sometimes it wasn't what people said to me, but how they said it. A few people spoke to me in a whisper or with a drawn out rhythm in their voice: "H-o-w a-r-e y-o-u d-o-i-n-g?" I was surprised they treated me more gingerly than before cancer. Maybe they just didn't know what to say. It was awkward. I didn't want to be treated any differently because I had cancer. I did not want anyone to pity or avoid me, just react toward me like they would anybody else. I had cancer, not the plague.

The only difference between me, a cancer survivor, and other people was I discovered it could happen to me; and they still think it will never happen to them. It is a different awareness, as well as experience.

Well, I believe they meant well, so rather than take offense to their remarks, I considered playing the …

OPPORTUNITY KNOCKED

I tested this strategy when I went to a camera store to return an expensive cable, and was told I would not get a refund because the seven-day grace period had passed. As the store manager turned to walk away from me, I blurted out, "I'm a Cancer Survivor!" and lifted my blouse to show him my huge, ugly scar.

I did that because the scar shows I've been hurt, the scar is evidence I've been healed, and the scar is empathy. Well, that man changed his tune pretty quick. And with his eyes wide open, he hastily gave me my forty dollars.

As I left the store, refund in hand, I thought *this cancer survivor thing isn't bad.* When I got home I stood in front of the mirror and lifted my blouse as I did in the store, to see what the manager saw that was so persuasive. To my horror, I realized I had inadvertently lifted my blouse too high. I flashed him. Well, I can never go back to that store again. Worse yet, now I'm not sure why I got the refund. (This could revolutionize shopping as we know it.)

TIP #12:

Forgive people for the stupid things they say in their attempt to comfort you in your difficult circumstance. And ignore any comments that may feed fear.

Chapter Eight

DON'T WALK AWAY FROM NEGATIVE PEOPLE ... RUN!

My cancer treatment included two major surgeries, six months apart, using the same big cut; five months of rigorous chemotherapy in between the surgeries; prayer, support of family and friends, watching funny movies every evening, and avoiding negative people.

Negative people, naysayers, even if they were related, could only bring me down and drain what little energy I had. It was imperative I only had contact with people who aided me to maintain a positive attitude throughout this difficult time.

POWER OF THE TONGUE

Words not only reflect our attitude, words can shape our attitude. Positive speech promotes a positive attitude; negative speech cultivates a negative attitude. What we hear, we repeat; and what we say, comes back to us. In other words, what we say is what we get, a self-fulfilling prophecy.

"The tongue has the power of life and death" (Proverbs 18:21). Those who say they can be healed of cancer and those who say they can't are both right. "Out of the same mouth comes blessing and cursing" (James 3:10). "Words are vessels. They convey fear or faith and they produce after their kind" (Capps, *The Tongue, Creative Force*).

Avoiding negative people's comments, like "Cancer always comes back" was key to fighting fear, which is produced by believing the wrong things. Fear is the reverse of faith. "Jesus said to His disciples, 'Why are you so afraid? Do you still have no faith?' " (Mark 4:40).

I didn't need more fear. Fear was easy. I had a diploma in fear. Having enough faith to survive was hard. The Word says, "We live by faith, not by sight" (2 Corinthians 5:7), but that was easier said than done under the circumstances. I struggled to focus on faith when I could not see ever living a normal life again.

ABOUT FAITH

"Now faith is being sure of what we hope for and certain of what we do not see" (Hebrews 11:1). Scripture further asserts all that is required is faith "as small as a mustard seed" (Matthew 17:20); but when fear crept in, my mustard seed faith was reduced to a speck. At times I relied solely upon the faith of others to pull me through the darkness.

I definitely needed an increase of faith in order to conquer fear, and trust in the Lord for my healing. According to God's Word, faith and healing go hand in hand: "Take heart, daughter, your faith has healed you" (Matthew 9:22). "Then Jesus touched their eyes and said, 'According to your faith will it be done to you' " (Matthew 9:29).

I sought faith. "... faith comes from hearing the message, and the message is heard through the word of Christ" (Romans 10:17).

The Lord put on a friend's heart to give me Dodie Osteen's book, *Healed of Cancer,* which includes forty scriptures stating God's power and desire to heal. I carried that little green book with me, and no matter how poorly I felt, I kept saying what the Word says until it became a part of me. Speaking God's words programmed my spirit, my heart, for success. It was the one-two punch that defended my faith.

Therefore, I prayed victory, not defeat; the solution, not the problem. I didn't deny the existence of cancer cells, but rather their right to continue in my body. Any negative prognosis was not allowed in my survival mind set; instead, I was focused on the promises of God concerning my healing. I believed "God's Word, conceived in my heart, then formed by my tongue, spoken out of my mouth, became a spiritual force releasing the ability of God within me" (Capps).

Because what we say can either foster faith or discourage it, there was absolutely no place in my treatment regimen for negative talkers. Including those who unintentionally planted seeds of doubt with their remarks, which the enemy used as fiery darts to destroy my hope.

For example, some people mistakenly thought they were saying something positive to me when they said, "Oh, you're in remission," which means a lessening or disappearance of symptoms. But the inference is that those symptoms may and probably will return. There's clearly nothing positive about the possibility or probability of that happening.

"No," I corrected, "I'm not in remission." And I stood on God's promise, "I'm healed by Jesus' stripes." (Isaiah 53:5, "But He was pierced for our transgressions, He was crushed for our iniquities; the punishment that brought us peace was upon Him, and by His wounds we are healed.")

Ephesians 6:16-17 says to be strong in the Lord's power and put on His armor to fight fear with faith: "Take up the shield of faith, with which you can extinguish all the flaming arrows of the evil one ... and take the sword of the Spirit, which is the Word of God." For example:

The fiery dart: "Doctors always say they got it all, but it comes back."

Nahum 1:9: "This trouble will not rise up a second time."

The fiery dart: "Three out of four ovarian cancer patients die."

2 Timothy 1:7: "For God did not give us a spirit of timidity, but spirit of power, of love, and of self-discipline."

The fiery dart: "Oh, that's the toughest cancer to beat. My mom died from ovarian cancer."

Proverbs 23:18: "There is surely a future hope for you, and your hope will not be cut off."

The fiery dart: "They say chemotherapy kills all your good cells too."

2 Chronicles 20:20: " ... have faith in the Lord your God and you will be upheld."

As I deflected attacks upon my faith with the Word, I had a mental image of Wonder Woman, my favorite DC Comics Super Heroine, who deflects bullets off the indestructible bracelets she wears by holding her arms out in front of her body. She is super cool, but the Shield of Faith is even more impressive.

TIP #13:

Extinguish the fiery darts of the enemy by countering with God's Word. For example, "God is our refuge and strength, an ever-present help in trouble." (Psalm 46:1)

TIP #14:

Watch your words. Positive speech promotes positive attitude, negative speech cultivates negative thinking. Pray victory, not defeat. "The tongue has the power of life and death." (Proverbs 18:21)

TIP #15:

Run from negative people. Even if they are blood related. I mean it.

Chapter Nine
THEY CALL THIS THERAPY?

Chemotherapy ... the cure some people say is "worse than the disease." I'd heard about the resulting nausea, vomiting, diarrhea, constipation, headache, weakness, fatigue, restlessness, neuropathy in fingers and toes, mouth sores, and some of these side effects in combination.

When I walked into the chemo clinic the first time, January 15, 2007, I didn't know if what I'd heard about chemo was true. In fact, I had no clue what to expect at my initial treatment. I was operating under the fear of the unknown.

The nurse directed me to sit in a chair next to the blood analysis machine. She pricked my finger and put my blood sample into that machine, which determined red and white blood cell counts. Based on the results, the nurse would either proceed to hook me up for infusion, or give me a shot to increase the blood count levels and reschedule the chemo session for another day. Despite being anemic, my blood levels fell within the allotted limits. The match was on. Round One.

The clinic was one large room with the nurses' stations in the middle, a smaller attached side room and tiled floors throughout. Around the perimeter along the walls were large recliner chairs in close proximity, and next to each recliner, a small chair or stool for visitors accompanying patients.

Mounted on the ceiling was a new television set that was turned off. When I asked a nurse about it, she said, "The TV is kept off to avoid patient arguments over channel selection." Although it seemed like a waste to me, I had to agree I wouldn't like being a captive audience forced to watch infomercials or the show about people shopping for houses. On second thought, I actually like the shows about people shopping for houses.

Blind-covered windows on the west wall afforded a limited view of the narrow parking lot that spanned the length of the building. Bookshelves near the entrance and nurses' station held some reading material, donated blankets and knit caps.

On top of one of the shelves was a box of free donuts, no doubt donated by a well-meaning individual. Because I'd recently read cancer loves sugar, I passed on the sugar-laden treat. Eating one donut may not have sabotaged my chemotherapy, but I didn't want to take the chance.

I chose a chair and waited for my turn to be hooked up to an I.V. bag. The needle was inserted and taped near the bend in my arm, making any movement painful. My infusion nurse, Andrea, put a pillow under my arm to ease my discomfort. Before the chemo drugs could be administered, she started me on steroids and anti-nausea drugs which she said would take about an hour.

Frank sat next to me on a folding chair while the oncology nurse, Sandra, stood over me, and read aloud the myriad of possible side effects of the chemo drugs that would soon be pumped into my vein. As she read the list in a routine, expressionless voice, I internalized my pleading—*I don't want to be here. I don't want to be here. I don't want to be here.*

I just couldn't believe I was actually hooked up to an I.V., and receiving chemotherapy. All I could think was, *this can't be happening to me.* I wanted to, no I considered, ripping that needle out of my arm and walking out of the clinic. I wanted to scream at her, "Stop reading those pronouncements over me!" I thought, *someone should tell her I don't belong here with cancer patients.*

That was the only time I had to fight back tears in the chemo clinic.

It was also the beginning of a long day. One of my drugs, Taxol, took two hours to drip, the other drug, Carboplatin, took four hours to drip. I called it a chemo marathon, but put a more positive spin on the extended treatment day by comparing it to an eight-hour work day. At the end of the day, I go home. Still, that was a long time to sit in a recliner without watching television.

All I brought to my first treatment was my insurance card. Food or drink never entered my mind. So when lunchtime came and Frank and I were both a little hungry, he went to a nearby deli to get sandwiches. Despite the anti-nausea medicine I'd received, the couple bites of sandwich I swallowed didn't settle well, so I gave up on eating.

As I looked around the room I noticed other patients brought large tote bags filled with snacks, such as crackers, fruit, Jell-O or pudding cups. Also water bottles or those little juice boxes with straws.

The bags were large enough to also hold a blanket, small pillow, books, knitting, iPods, journals. I made a mental note, next time I would come to chemo treatment prepared.

It was easy slipping into the comfortable recliners, getting out of them was another thing. The hand mechanism, which when pulled returned the leg rest to an upright position, was too stiff for me to pull. Someone had to come and get me out of the chair. Worse yet, a couple of the recliners retracted with such force and recoil I was catapulted out of the chair and onto the floor.

Therefore, I only got up during the day to go to the restroom, which wasn't easy because I had to hold on to the I.V. pole and drag it along as I walked.

INFUSION'S JUST STEP ONE

At the end of the day I was sent home with printed instructions, including remedies for side effects. For example, Zofran for nausea, Senecot for the constipation that resulted from taking Zofran, Compazine—another anti-nausea drug—which may be taken between the Zofran doses if Zofran didn't do the trick, Benadryl to calm the restlessness caused by the steroids, Lomitil for diarrhea and GasX for the gas, which was pervasive.

The trick to getting through chemotherapy was managing the multiple symptoms by juggling the ill effects with meds and other remedies. But no matter how good I was at that, I still felt like I had the flu—all day, everyday. I was weak and just wanted to go to bed and sleep through the next few days. But I couldn't. I had to stay up and force myself to eat something and drink water whether I felt like it or not.

Some of the meds were taken with food, others on an empty stomach. It was a full-time record-keeping job to track side effects, food and liquid intake, medications, and reactions. I kept a notebook on the kitchen counter for that purpose.

Most important was the instruction to drink ninety-six ounces of water each day for the first seventy-two hours following chemotherapy. That's nine glasses of water. The handout said "to protect the kidneys." I tried to drink as much as I could, but I couldn't force down that much water each day.

Later I read a medical report in a magazine which warned that cancer cells being flushed out of the body may settle into the kidneys, and cause kidney cancer if the patient fails to drink the recommended amount of water. So what I thought was just a recommendation, was actually a warning of a potentially serious consequence of chemotherapy, more cancer! Great.

VIRTUALLY FORCED FEEDING

Eating enough food to keep up my strength was a problem because I did not feel hungry at all. And the less I ate, the weaker I became. I decided I was not going to waste away during the months of chemotherapy. That meant I would plan ahead and have some nutritious snacks readily available to me.

I also put Frank on alert after the first time he asked me if I'd eaten anything and, when I told him no, he turned and walked out of the room. I called him back and told him to not take no for an answer, but stop and bring me a handful of food and make me eat it before he walked away, or I feared I would die from starvation.

The drugs I was given changed my taste buds as well as my appetite. My heart was warmed by the meals friends prepared and brought over for my family, but I could not eat the dishes because they were too spicy for me to tolerate.

The key was to find foods I could stomach, then force myself to eat a little bit whether I felt hungry or not. What worked for me was one scrambled egg, or one-fourth of a plain chicken sandwich (the canned chicken from Costco), one tablespoon of peanut butter, yogurt, Jell-O or pudding.

Both my oncologist and his nurses said I could call anytime if I had a question. So when 11:30 p.m. came and I was still too restless from the steroids to sleep, I called to ask what I could do about it? The doctor assured me I was experiencing a normal reaction to the drugs, and he said I could take two Benadryl to help me fall asleep.

This would not be the last time I'd call the oncologist between treatments to verify the reactions and side effects I was experiencing were to be expected.

The first day of chemo, I left the clinic charged up on steroids and anti-nausea medicine. The sick feeling and side effects didn't really kick in until the second day after treatment. Then it was worse the third day, and the fourth, and the fifth, and the sixth, and the seventh day.

After the first week, I turned a corner and started feeling slightly better each day. The second week after chemo was better than the first week, and by the third week I felt better still. Then it was time to go do it all over again. Once every three weeks for five months.

One chemotherapy round down, five to go.

TIP #16:

Refuse to receive fear. Fear does not come from the Lord. "God did not give us a spirit of timidity, but a spirit of power, of love, and of self-discipline" (2 Timothy 1:7). Rebuke fear in the name of Jesus.

Chapter Ten
HAVE BAG, WILL TRAVEL

CHEMO#2, February 6, 2007, I showed up for my second chemotherapy session better prepared. First, I made sure I was dressed for comfort. I wore a soft cotton velour warm up suit, which was given to me by my friend, Elizabeth, a red T-shirt with letters made of rhinestones across the chest that read HARDCORECHRISTIANCHICK, and a cozy fleece cap.

Secondly, I brought my own color-coordinated "Chemo Bag," as I called it, which I designed for maximum comfort and utility during chemo-therapy

The large, red vinyl tote bag included a soft lap-throw blanket, insulated lunch bag, travel cup, note pad/pen, an iPod, Dodie Osteen's pocket-size book *Healed of Cancer*, my camera to document the session, juice boxes, peanut butter, crackers, and a cuddly red bear Beany Baby.

Another thing I brought to chemo #2 was my friend and leader of Women's Ministries at my church, JoAnn Lee. She'd asked if she could go to my chemo treatment to keep me company. Luckily, I'd thrown an extra juice box into my bag for just such an occasion. JoAnn was the shot in the (other) arm that I needed.

As usual, JoAnn was enthusiasm in capris as she greeted me in her manner: "WELL, HOW IS MISS JANA THIS MORNING?!!"

Sometimes I wondered if that was a trick question.

There was a big crowd in the clinic that day, so I had to take a recliner in the smaller room. They call it "the quiet room," for patients who do not wish to be social during the time they are being infused. They read or sleep or just sit in silence, for hours.

Being relegated to the quiet room for the day was torture for me. JoAnn and I still enjoyed our conversation, although I did notice a couple of the quiet ones giving a side glance in the direction of my recliner now and then. We tried to keep our voices down, but I'm afraid our laughter bounced off the tile floor and then from wall to wall within that little room.

Each chemotherapy treatment affected me a little differently. Or more accurately, with each chemo came new side effects. Following chemo #2, I noticed I had become extremely sensitive to ordinary smells like cologne, scented lotions, deodorant, hair and skin care products. Just a whiff made me nauseous. In future, I had to ask my visitors to not use these products before coming to visit me.

BAD NEWS DIDN'T SIT WELL

I was home alone, seated at the kitchen table and trying to force down a half sandwich, when the phone rang. It was the ovarian cancer specialist from the Cedars-Sinai Medical Center Cancer Institute in Los Angeles, calling with the results of my PETT Scan.

She told me the image showed "a spot near the spleen" she believed was cancer, and she recommended I fly down to Los Angeles A.S.A.P. for surgery to remove it. I was devastated. Her words knocked me to the mat.

When I hung up the phone I burst into tears. I couldn't believe what I had just heard. She said they found more cancer in my body. What made the news worse, I was all alone when I received it.

Frank was out to lunch with our granddaughter, Cory, who had been working for him in his home office. They returned from their break to find me sobbing at the kitchen table. After I had calmed down enough to tell them about the bad news, cooler heads prevailed.

We jumped into the car and went to see my local surgeon. She told us, when she removed the omentum from where it connects to the spleen, bleeding resulted and she stopped the blood by putting what she called "surgical Super Glue" on that spot. She said the glue would eventually just dissolve in my body.

My surgeon called the Los Angeles doctor and explained that the image detected in the PETT scan undoubtedly was the glue. She followed up by faxing a copy of my surgical report along with a letter from the Physician Assistant stating she, too, specifically remembered the "surgical Super Glue" incident.

For weeks after that call I jumped every time the phone rang.

THE BIG CHEESE

With two of the six chemo treatments under my belt, it was time for Frank and me to travel to U.C.S.F Helen Diller Cancer Center in San Francisco to meet my gynecologic oncologist for the first time. Very bright, one of the "elitists" in the field, as the Newport Beach doctor testified. We were duly impressed by the doctor's credentials, and with utmost respect and admiration, I privately gave her the special moniker of "The Big Cheese."

As the other two ovarian cancer specialists did on our January trip to Southern California, the U.C.S.F. doctor reviewed my records, the CT scans (pelvic, abdominal, and thorax), and examined me before sitting down to talk with us about my prognosis. We asked the same questions we'd asked the other two gynecologic oncologists.

Most importantly, "Will the operation and five months of chemotherapy cure me, or only buy me some time?" Without hesitating, Doctor responded, "Buy you some time." She did give us a straightforward answer to our direct question but I thought, *gee, at least spin some hope on the end of it.*

I felt my brain start to shut down again, but I did hear the tag line. "It's the feisty ones who make it," she added. "And, in that regard, you are not at all the typical patient." I took that as a compliment, and I'd suspected it was the closest I'd get to a spin of hope on the end of the diagnosis. I decided not to ask what she meant by that. It was a straw and I grabbed it.

TIP #17:

Don't go it alone. Tell friends, family, church leaders what you're going through so they can offer assistance. Seek support from other Christian believers. They are the ones who will stand in the gap for you, and lift you up in intercessory prayer.

TIP #18:

Be the feisty one. Fight fear, don't surrender to it.

Chapter Eleven

NO ONE TOLD ME I WOULD LOSE MY EYEBROWS

CHEMO #3, February 27, 2007, was different right from the start. The mood in my half of the clinic was different, more lively. Three women were busy chattering about chemotherapy, even making light of our situation. I listened to the more experienced cancer patients, hoping to glean whatever I could that would help me become the Super Patient.

Sitting directly across from me was an older woman in her late 70's who periodically looked up from her newspaper to offer a comment. I was surprised when she said she'd been on chemotherapy continually for over four years, and had learned how to accept the regular treatments as a part of her life's routine.

The most memorable moment came when she prefaced her offering with these words, "Girls, the most important thing you need to know about chemotherapy," then paused. I thought, *This is it. This is the tidbit I was hoping for. The one piece of information that will give me the knowledge and understanding I need to survive the dreaded chemotherapy.*

I held my breath so no internal noise would interfere with my reception of her sage advice as she continued, "Always remember ... don't ever leave home without your eyebrows."

Eyebrows? That's it? What does she mean, "Don't ever leave home without your eyebrows"? Then it hit me. *I'm going to lose my eyebrows!* I'll be reduced to drawing their replica on my forehead with a makeup pencil.

The doctor told me one of the two drugs I was taking would cause hair loss, but he never mentioned I would also lose my eyebrows! Why wasn't that critical information included in the side effects handout? That should have been in the handout.

And why the heck didn't my oncologist tell me this important piece of chemo information? Instead, I had to hear the news from another cancer patient, the experienced woman who seemed to take it all in stride, the lady who's neatly penciled eyebrows stood out as she peeked over the top of her newspaper.

Another cancer patient offered tips on how to make hair grow back more quickly following months of chemotherapy treatment. She said someone told her they heard we could stimulate hair re-growth by rubbing a piece of Velcro on our scalps.

Granted, Velcro is a useful product, some may even say a modern marvel, but that's the point at which I dropped out of the group conversation. From that day on, I took the advice I heard from other patients in the clinic with a grain a salt.

THE ACCIDENTAL APPOINTMENTS

The effects of chemo were cumulative, magnifying fatigue with each new treatment. Chemo #3 was also different from sessions #1 and #2, because three days following infusion I lacked the strength to even sit up or stand. I literally crawled. When Frank entered the room and discovered me, alarmed he asked, "What are you doing on the floor?"

It was very frightening for us both. I suspected something had gone terribly wrong, and feared my body would not be able to tolerate the three remaining treatments. Worse yet, perhaps chemo had gotten the best of me. Maybe the cure, not the disease, would kill me.

My blood pressure had dropped to 90/40, and Frank took me in to see my oncologist without an appointment. The doctor explained to us chemo drugs can lower blood pressure. He said people who take medicine for high blood pressure can sometimes be taken off those drugs while on chemo. The down side is people like me who ordinarily have perfect 110/70, can experience a dramatic drop in blood pressure.

The solution was to hydrate me by hooking me up to an I.V. with saline drip. The infusion clinic was over-crowded that Friday, so the staff was hard-pressed to make a place to squeeze me in for two hours. After that day, I always made a standing appointment to be hydrated three days following infusion. If I felt alright on the third day, I called and cancelled the appointment. This new backup plan covered me, and did not inconvenience or overtax the staff at the clinic.

HAIR TODAY, GONE TOMORROW

I believe most women would agree the worst part of chemo was losing hair. I hated to lose my hair. It was upsetting, emotional, demoralizing, humiliating. And I'm just talking about the bangs.

I dreaded the trauma of dropping clumps of hair around the house. I wanted to decide when and how I would lose my hair; so I went to my hairdresser, Judi, to help me with that painful transition. I think it went pretty well ...

... All I said to her was, "Just take a little bit off the sides."

SOON CHEMO TOOK ITS TOLL

To look in the mirror and see a bald woman staring back was a shock and a reminder of the gravity of my illness. I don't think my family knew how much time I spent in the bathroom, closely examining  my shiny, hairless head in the magnifying mirror I used to apply make up. I contemplated, *How strange that person in the mirror looks, and who is she?* as I repeatedly ran my hand over my smooth, bald scalp. Cancer not only made me unrecognizable, cancer made me disappear.

"Lord, are you still with me?" I asked aloud. "I feel so isolated." I reminded Him of His Word (Romans 8:35 & 37): "You said, 'Who shall separate us from the love of Christ? Shall trouble or hardship' (and, boy, this situation sure qualifies) ... 'No, in all these things we are more than conquerors through Him who loved us.' So, God, help me feel like the conqueror you say I am, even if I don't feel like a conqueror, or see one when I look in the mirror."

When I got down to only one eyelash, I was scared to death I would never be normal again. I reached deep inside for the faith that God would not abandon me in that valley. Not immediately, but soon, I realized His love had lifted me up, comforted me and given me a cheerful heart.

"A cheerful heart is good medicine," (Proverbs 17:22). I was able to laugh at the situation and find the funny in my fight against cancer. I made the decision not to mourn the loss of my eyelashes, but to celebrate that one remaining lash. I curled it, and put mascara on it. It was sure easy getting ready in the morning.

PAIN INTO GAIN

I suspected God probably wouldn't waste this traumatic experience; instead, he'd somehow redeem the suffering and use the testimony to touch others. I remembered one night in 1979, single and alone in my apartment, watching Christian television, when I asked God to use me; but I didn't recall signing up for this. Ovarian cancer was not what I had in mind.

I was thinking more along the lines of a less painful and much less frightening life experience which might inspire a muffin ministry:

6.4

TIP #19:

Reach out to God. Call upon Him and He will answer. "So do not fear, for I am with you; do not be dismayed, for I am your God. I will strengthen you and help you; I will uphold you with my righteous right hand." (Isaiah 41:10)

TIP #20:

Hug your hair dresser. Just because.

Chapter Twelve

GOD TOOK ME BACK TO BRING ME FORWARD

That night in 1979, I saw Vietnam veteran Dave Roever's appearance on The Trinity Broadcasting Network. He sat in a wheelchair as he recounted his story of how God brought him through a horrific battle experience, long painful recuperation and reconstruction, and living with permanent impairments.

While on patrol in a small boat, he was hit by a sniper as he was about to throw a phosphorous grenade, which then exploded in his hand. His right ear, eye, hand, and the right side of his face were blown off, and his body set ablaze. Dave described himself as "burned to a crisp."

His fellow soldiers thought he was dead as he floated in shallow water next to his own skin and separated body parts. I was glued to the television as Roever joked, "I was beside myself. I had to pull myself together."

FLASHBACK

I never forgot what Dave related next. In that unimaginable moment in Vietnam that changed his life forever, he came up out of the water and affirmed, "God, I still love you." His declaration gave me pause. I wasn't sure I could love God that much if I were to so suffer.

Moved and convicted by Dave's testimony, I asked God, "Give me faith like Dave Roever's faith." Then I sealed my fate by petitioning the Lord to "Give me a testimony like Dave Roever's." By the end of Dave's televised segment I told God, "I want a ministry like Dave Roever's," not realizing the ramification of what I was desiring. I didn't grasp it then, but that was a crossroad in my Christian walk. That was also the first and last time I saw Dave Roever on television.

FLASH FORWARD 2007

My family relocated from Southern California to the Central Valley of the northern part of the state. As I was reading the weekly bulletin in church one Sunday, I was surprised to see the announcement: Dave Roever would be coming to my town, to my church. God instantly called to my memory that night when I watched Dave testify on television.

I told my husband about Dave Roever, and how the Lord used him to touch my heart so many years before. I revealed to Frank that my first spoken words when I awoke alone in my hospital room after surgery, in great pain and on fire, were Dave's affirmation of faith, "God, I still love you." I told Frank that after I uttered those words in the hospital, tears rolled down my cheeks, because I realized I had the strong, solid, relationship with the Lord I desired and asked Him for years ago. In that epiphanic moment, I felt I passed my self-imposed test of faith.

AN ORDAINED MEETING

After church I called Pastor Edwards at home, recounted what Dave Roever meant to me, and asked if I could meet with the guest speaker

in his office prior to the start of church service. He agreed to the meeting. As we posed for this photo, Dave said, "Like the name of your ministry, we have both Been There – Got The Wig!"®

I excitedly told Dave how his testimony impacted my life, way back when I was in my twenties; and I thanked him for his faithfulness to be used of God by telling his story. I told him about asking God to give me a ministry like his, adding I had no idea what I was really asking for at the time. The adage "be careful what you pray for" held new meaning. Dave nodded with understanding.

He said, "Years ago I did the same thing. As I sat in Dave Wilkerson's audience, I said to myself, 'I could do what Wilkerson does. I'd like to have a ministry like his,' not realizing what that meant."

How about that. Roever and I had a similar pivotal moment in our lives. And admittedly, we were both naive about what we were getting ourselves into.

After identifying myself to Dave as an Inspirational Humorist, briefly telling of my cancer surgery and treatment, and speaking of the Been There – Got The Wig!® Breakfast Club, I told Dave that he has a part of this ministry. He responded with a big smile, "I'll be happy to have a piece of that ministry."

GOD USES DAVE ROEVER AGAIN

My professional background is in broadcast journalism in Hollywood, where cut-throat competitors steal ideas, program content, and fail to give credit where due. So what Dave did next really surprised and blessed me.

He gave me a signature piece to include in my presentations. Dave looked me in the eye and pointed at me as he pronounced, "This is for you. You use this: your scar shows you've been hurt, your scar is evidence you've been healed, your scar is empathy." He added, "Don't be afraid to let it show. Someone who hurts will see themselves in you. You can touch another heart."

As I left Pastor's office and took my seat in the church sanctuary, I thought, *Okay God, so twenty-seven years ago you used this Vietnam vet to speak into my life, then nearly three decades later our paths cross in a small town in Northern California, and again you used him to speak into my life. Now I want you to verify what Dave told me today was from you. I need to know you really did heal me, and you have a specific plan for my life post cancer.*

I sat in the front row, and before Dave began to address the crowd, I put out a fleece, so to speak. I prayed under my breath: "Lord, if Dave is here to confirm you healed me, for your glory, for your purposes, and for a Been There ministry, then cause him to stop in the middle of his planned presentation, and call me up on stage to tell me so."

Well, Dave did not stop in the middle of his presentation and call me up on stage. He stopped in the middle of his presentation, and without explanation he walked down the steps of the stage, crossed the floor to where I sat, and stood a foot in front of me. Face-to-face and on mic he spoke prophetically to me as the audience listened, unaware of my prayer request.

"God's gonna give you something that's going to change your world. He trusted you with a scar that's gonna turn a life—don't hide the scar. Because somebody out there has been hurt just like you, and you're the only Jesus they're gonna find who has a scar like yours."

Then Dave returned to the stage and resumed his presentation from the point that he had interrupted himself to deliver a personal message from God to me. Wow. Frank also knew we had just witnessed a special move of the Holy Spirit. We both shed tears of awe and gratitude to God. Our pastor, who was seated on the side of the stage, grinned as we locked eyes and he pointed to me energetically.

To everyone else in church that day, Roever was probably just another guest speaker. But to me, the messenger's presence alone was also the message. God could have used anyone to confirm my healing and validate my future, but He didn't. God sent the same guy He used in 1979, because that triggered my memory of the encounter God and I had years ago, an encounter which only the two of us knew about.

By sending Dave, the Lord proved He hadn't forgotten me. God spoke into my heart, "I heard you that night alone in your apartment, and I hear you now. And so you'll know you did hear from me regarding your healing and the ministry which is yours, I sent my same servant as years ago to testify to you today."

It was like receiving a postcard from God. That was the shot of hope I needed to believe I had a future, and the boost in courage I needed to continue on.

My immediate future included proceeding with the second half of my chemotherapy treatments—numbers four, five and six.

TIP #21:

Don't underestimate God. He is always one step ahead of us. Maybe more. He has a great memory, too.

TIP #22:

Be careful what you pray for. Make you dream big enough for God to fit into, then step back.

Chapter Thirteen
CHEMO BRAIN & OTHER NEW SIDE EFFECTS

CHEMO #4, March 20, 2007. Because I believe what you speak is what you get, I was careful not to claim the so-called chemo brain, "a mental fog caused by any one or combination of factors, such as stress, fatigue, anti-nausea or pain medications." If I had trouble remembering details, or concentrating, or was slower thinking, I was quick to explain it's not chemo brain . . . I'm just old. *Oh, wait a minute.*

I still had a good memory, but it had become considerably and noticeably shorter. For example, I found it difficult to write in my notes, because I repeatedly lost my train of thought. I spent more time and energy trying to recall what I planned to write rather than composing the content. The exercise left me mentally drained and my notebook pages relatively empty.

I also had a hard time memorizing my new cell phone number. Frequently I transposed the last four digits which were: 5-0-3-8. So to remember the correct sequence, I recited this phrase: "I used to be 50 years old, and I've never had a 38" bust."

This memory technique worked just fine for me until my friend, Carole, brought to my attention it is also true I used to be 38 years old, and I've never had a 50" bust.

THEY WERE HERE SOMEWHERE

The task of restoring my facial features robbed by chemo, proved to be another mental challenge. After fifty-seven years of looking at my own face in the mirror, I assumed I would remember where my eyebrows used to be. But apparently when I lost my brows, along with them went my memory. Their exact location escaped me as I attempted to draw eyebrows on my forehead freehand with a make-up pencil.

Luckily, I found an eyebrow stencil at a Sephora make-up store. The pre-cut template stuck to my forehead, and I just filled in the eyebrow-shaped pattern. The key to using this technique was to remember the correct placement of the left and right template, which I occasionally forgot. An inadvertent switching of the two patterns gave me the startled look of someone being interrogated by the IRS over their tax deductions.

BRAIN FREEZE

Sometimes it was tough to focus my attention, yet at other times my brain would be stuck on a single thought. For example, when one song stuck in my head and I couldn't resist singing the lyrics aloud, over and over and over again, day and night, driving myself and everyone around me crazy. I just couldn't help myself. I was held captive by this annoying tune: "Macho Macho Man. I want to be a Macho Man. Macho Macho Man. I want to be a Macho Man. Macho Macho Man. I want to be a Macho Man. Macho Macho Man. I want to be a Macho Man. Macho Macho Man. I want to be" . . .

The variety of drugs I was taking also gave me unusual dreams. In a feeble attempt to understand the mini-series that played in my head as I slept, I surveyed one of those *How To Interpret Your Dreams* books. I was especially interested in deciphering one of my recurring dreams starring actor Harrison Ford. No matter how many times I had that dream, it always ended the same.

Harrison Ford begged me to leave town with him and I resisted. I did. I honestly did. My mother would have been proud of me—I resisted over-packing for the trip. My mom taught me to lay out the clothes I wanted to take, and then put half of them back in the closet. Not surprisingly, I found no reference to this sequence in the book of dream interpretations.

MORE SIDE EFFECTS

Also new with this chemo treatment was neuropathy in fingers and toes, as well as increased fatigue. I lacked the energy to even dress myself or apply make-up. Furthermore, for the first time in my life, I didn't care how I looked. I had reached an all-time low in personal pride.

I only stepped out of the house to go to doctor appointments, to which I commonly wore pj's, slippers, a terry cloth turban, no bra, no underwear and no make-up. Yeah, my appearance was scary. My only hope was I looked so bad I was rendered unrecognizable.

Although Mom always told me emphatically, "Don't even walk to the mail box without at least putting on some lipstick," the fatigue caused me to be unresponsive to this ingrained vanity.

NOT WHAT I HAD EXPECTED

Between CHEMO #4 and CHEMO #5 was another milestone. Our silver wedding anniversary. Months before cancer, we had reserved a condo on the beach in Maui, Hawaii. We usually commemorated anniversaries with just a simple dinner for two at a great restaurant; but this was to be our special week of celebrating us, and our twenty-five years of marriage.

We had to make a decision quickly or lose our deposit. Frank still wanted us to go to Maui that week, so he pointed out the dates of the trip would fall between my scheduled treatments.

I explained I wasn't supposed to be in intense sun during the months I was on chemo. Also, if we traveled at that time, I would be an invalid rather than a tourist. I'd have no energy to walk on the beach or go into the water. Not to mention, I'd be bald in a bikini. Being sick and miserable in Maui's hot, humid, climate was certainly not my idea of our dream silver anniversary trip.

We were both disappointed when we cancelled the Hawaiian vacation, but fortunately, we were able to get back our deposit.

Plan B: Instead, on our anniversary we drove to San Francisco to see my gynecologic oncologist. Per usual for my office visits to the doctor, I stripped down and was partially covered by a short paper gown as I lay on the exam table with my feet in the stirrups. Frank sat on the other side of a curtain in a chair by the door. Well, at least one of us was naked. Still, this wasn't the way I'd always imagined our 25th wedding anniversary celebration.

We spent the remainder of the day driving around the Bay Area and taking pictures together. I didn't want the memory of our silver anniversary to be just about doctor visits and exams, so I planned ahead. I brought the wooden numerals 2 and 5, which I had spray painted silver. Ta-da ...

... Instant alternative anniversary memory.

SMILING THROUGH THE PAIN

CHEMO #5, April 10, 2007, was like the four previous treatments, only more so. Cumulative fatigue, headache, nausea, constipation, diarrhea, gas, neuropathy. The trick to getting through chemotherapy was managing meds to balance the various side effects.

Actually, it was more of a juggling act as I had to choose the lesser of two evils at any given time throughout the day. My choice was often made by asking questions: would I rather be less nauseated, but constipated? Or vice versa?"

BEEN THERE . . .

GOT THE WIG! ®

Years ago, being caught wearing a wig was a negative. They were stiff, too thick, old, out-dated styles that looked like fake hair. Today's wigs come in a greater variety of contemporary styles, with fluid movement, and more natural colors. These modern wigs are often worn undetected.

Over the duration of my chemo treatments, I acquired 3 different colors and styles of wigs, and alternated wearing them to fit my mood.

Black & White

Medium Brown

Dark Brown
(Gloves Optional)

Once I embraced the convenience of a wig, I wondered why I hadn't thought of buying a wig decades ago to eliminate bad hair days.

Five Chemo treatments down, only ONE more to go!

TIP #23:

Always have a Plan B. A little bit of preplanning can change a negative experience into a positive memory.

TIP #24:

Always put on lipstick before walking to the mailbox. Mother was right.

Chapter Fourteen

A CHEERFUL HEART IS GOOD MEDICINE

CHEMO # 6, May 1, 2007, the ill effects of chemo continued for days, and even weeks beyond each treatment. At times the cure did seem worse than the disease. As I grew physically weaker and weaker throughout the five months of chemotherapy, I continued to fight fear. In that weakened state I could understand how it would be so easy to want to just give up and throw in the towel.

It was only because I believed God loves me, and I had faith in His Word, that I was able to find the strength and courage I needed to not throw in the towel, hang in there and make it to my 6th and final chemo treatment.

To celebrate this victory of completing treatment, some patients bring flowers or balloons with them to the chemo clinic. For me, it was clearly a day to wear what I call my Celebration Glasses. (I always carry them in the trunk of my car, just in case.)

My regular nurse, Andrea, was absent the day of my last chemo, so another infusion nurse assisted me. At the end of the day as she unhooked the I.V. drip for the last time, she said to me, "Well you're all done, we won't be seeing you again." I didn't understand the contradiction of prognosis.

I am the positive attitude lady, but everything I'd read about ovarian cancer reported there is no cure. Instead, an anticipated life span of only two to four years including recurrence requiring heavier chemo, more surgeries, followed by another recurrence and even heavier chemo, and then I die. So I responded, "But I had ovarian cancer."

"Oh, we've had lots of ovarian cancer survivors who have never needed to come back for more chemotherapy," was her cheerful reply. I was flabbergasted, "Why didn't somebody tell me that five months ago when I started chemo?"

"We're not allowed to say because of the new privacy laws," she explained.

"Well, I'm not asking for names." I qualified, "It just would have been nice to know. I would have been more encouraged. More hopeful."

But maybe then I might not have fought so hard against fear, nor sought the Lord as diligently and, as a result, my faith would not have been increased. Perhaps if I'd known going into this difficult struggle survival was a possibility, however slight, I would not be as close to the Lord today. The process of going through this hardship not only changed my life, it changed my heart.

A CHEERFUL HEART DEMONSTRATED

My long and emotional seven-hour chemo sessions were every three weeks from January to May. In that time I got so attached to that I.V. pole, that I bought it and modified it by attaching a few of my favorite things. Now I take the pole with me to speaking engagements and demonstrate its alternative uses. I ring the bicycle bell if I'm in heavy foot traffic.

The plaques remind me: "A day without laughter is a day wasted." And "Never, Never, Never Give Up!"

My infusion nurses really loved my little sound-effects machine.

I pushed the button for the sound of a woman screaming as the nurse stuck me with the needle. And at the end of the day when she removed the needle, I hit the button for the canned laughter.

Like a lot of people, I take my water bottle with me wherever I go.

Now that I'm fully recuperated and up 'n' around, I use the clip to attach my water bottle to my belt loop. It's very handy. People barely notice it.

To commemorate the milestone of my final chemo, my husband gave me a special gift he picked out himself. It was a DVD:

I don't see that happening.

The DVD came with a bonus gift . . .

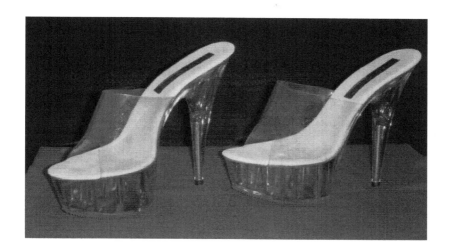

It was really hard to stand in these. My husband fell down twice.

TIP #25:

Strength comes from the Lord, "but those who hope in the Lord will renew their strength" (Isaiah 40:31).

TIP #26:

Never, never, never give up! Winston Churchill said, "When you're going through hell, keep going."

Chapter Fifteen
NOT THAT AGAIN!

Worse than chemo and cancer was the pain, suffering, and l-o-n-g recuperation following surgery. The last thing I wanted to do was repeat that experience. But the fact my initial surgery was not performed by a gynecologic oncologist and, subsequently, my lymph nodes in the lower abdominal and pelvic region were left intact, gave me pause and could signal possible disaster in the future.

Gynecologic oncologists I interviewed told me they are of the school of thought to always remove and biopsy the nodes, regardless of their appearance, because they've found there is a thirty percent chance they harbor microscopic cancer cells which may metastasize later.

A thirty percent chance the nodes were "dirty" means there's seventy percent chance they were "clean." That's roughly one chance out of three I still had cancer inside me, but two chances out of three I did not. It sounded like the odds were in my favor. And yet, I never thought I would be that one woman out of three to get cancer in the first place. I wasn't willing to gamble my future on the percentages.

Some ovarian cancer patients choose to have a "second-look surgery," as it is called, which is performed after a procedure or course of treatment (chemo) to determine if the patient is free of disease. If disease is found, additional procedures may or may not be performed at the time of the second-look surgery.

Again, I was in the position of gathering information to aid me (us) in making the decision whether or not to take the risks that would accompany another major surgery for the sake of a second look.

102 | Jana Flaig

Opinions varied.

I spoke on the phone with a representative of the National Ovarian Cancer Alliance. She offered her personal opinion, urging me to not go under the knife again, citing basic dangers of surgical procedures.

Then there was Rene, a Christian lady with whom I shared several chemotherapy sessions. She had the same cancer, same surgery as I did, including not removing the lymph nodes. She told me she regretted not opting for the second-look surgery at the time, because as it turned out, her nodes did have microscopic cancer, which grew and spread to other organs throughout her body. When Rene and I met she had been on chemotherapy non-stop for more than three years, and was wasting away.

I'll never forget the day we sat side by side in our chemo recliners and she looked me in the eye and pleaded, "Knowing what I know now, have the surgery, Jana." My friend, Rene, died soon after that. She never knew that her words may have saved my life.

I'LL TAKE THE BULLET HOLES, PLEASE

I really didn't want to go down that major surgery road again, especially after only six months since the first surgery. But Frank and I were in agreement we had to do everything we could do, including more surgeries, more chemo if needed, in order to give me the best chance at survival. I had no choice but to jump back into the ring.

One month after my last chemo treatment, I checked into the Zion Medical Center at U.C.S.F. for my second-look surgery with high hopes. I hoped the nodes could be taken by a minimally invasive procedure, I'd be out of the hospital the next day, and my family wouldn't have to spend a week in a nearby apartment.

The plan was The Big Cheese would first try laparoscopic techniques, making small half-inch incisions to look inside the abdomen and to remove lymph nodes from my pelvic region. This would leave me with only a few "bullet holes," as they are called by the medical staff.

The operative word here was "try" this technique, because it provided the doctor a restricted access and a limited view. She forewarned me, if it were so determined at the time of surgery, I would be opened up using the same big cut as the first operation. The possibility of that made me cringe, *Oh no, not that again!*

Obviously, we prayed the bullet holes would do the trick, affording me considerably less pain and suffering, and time spent in the hospital. Needless to say, I desperately wanted to be spared a sequel operation, followed by another month in a rented hospital bed at home. Nevertheless, I told God if there is something inside my body that would not be revealed to the doctor unless she opened me up all the way, then let it be.

When I awoke in my hospital room after surgery, I saw I had bullet holes, AND a big cut from my pelvic bone all the way up to my ribs. The good news was the large incision was closed with only twenty staples this time. I couldn't help but think of the surgeon's assistant who closed my incision in the first operation using eighty staples. *Maybe she should consider switching to decaf.*

OOPS, WHAT'S THAT DOING THERE?

I wondered why I had to be opened up again. The doctor later explained, during the laparoscopic procedure the device "bumped into a section of the colon which was not where it was supposed to be, due to scar tissue resulting from the first surgery." Consequently, she had to open me up all the way to remove four to five inches of my transverse colon.

My doctor added, "The tissue was very unhealthy." I asked, "How unhealthy was it?" and was told, "Very unhealthy." I pressed for more detail because I needed to know just how far I could embellish my surgery story. "Was it gangrene?"

"No. But it was very unhealthy." I took that to mean if I hadn't chosen to have the second-look surgery, which revealed a portion of my colon was in the wrong place with unhealthy deteriorating tissue, that unseen condition would have eventually killed me. My interpretation of these remarks wasn't based so much on her words, as it was her facial expression of repulsion each time the doctor described the removed section as "very unhealthy."

LIKE NIGHT & DAY

Even though my hospitalization was longer than I had hoped for, this time my hospital stay went much better than my first experience, and I got out two days earlier for good behavior. Happily, I was in a large room by myself, and I'm sure it helped that I had a better idea of what to expect during those five days. Additionally, I was no longer anemic so I went into this operation physically stronger.

It wasn't any easier to pull myself up and out of bed, or to walk with the assistance of a walker, or go to the restroom while attached to an I.V. pole; but having gained a different mind-set over the past six months, and a renewed confidence in my relationship with the Lord, I felt more dread than fear.

Frank was able to rent a two bedroom suite in an extended stay apartment complex within two blocks of the hospital. When he and Luke were not sitting at my bedside, they were able to enjoy many of the comforts of home.

Being a patient in the hospital can rob one's identity. I didn't want to be just another faceless person in a hospital gown. I wanted the nurses to know Jana; to see me as I used to be before cancer treatments aged my skin and turned my hair, which was growing back, from salt & pepper to mostly salt.

Fortuitously, I had a six inch diameter photo button of me in healthier days, which I had taken at a county fair years prior because I thought it might come in handy some day. The image bore virtually no resemblance to the weakened lady sleeping in the bed. It was just another attempt to regain the me before cancer.

I pinned the button to my hospital gown, and I also wore it on the front of my robe when I walked the hallways.

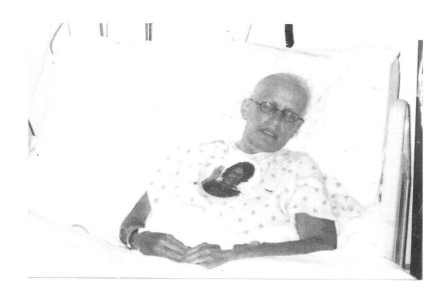

I planned ahead and brought my mirror ball disco earrings to wear when I took my post surgery exercise walk up and down the hall.

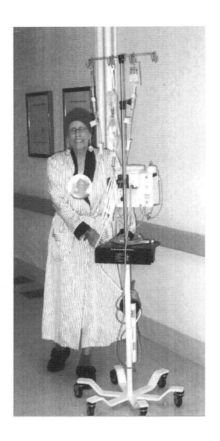

You never know when the hospital Public Relations photographer is roaming the halls, looking for subjects to include in the new hospital brochures.

SHORT TERM GOAL

As a Cancer Survivor, and all-around over-achiever, I wanted to be the doctor's and the nurses' favorite patient. I strived to be that one patient who not only politely followed their instructions, and expressed appreciation for their attention, but also made their day by sharing entertaining stories or quips. I wanted to be that patient. I wanted to be the best patient I could be. I wanted to be ...

The SUPER PATIENT

TO THAT END

I made a concerted effort to ensure the hospital staff was fully aware of my dedication and willingness to take their direction. For example, in order to remove congestion from my lungs and prevent pneumonia after surgery, I was told to do deep breathing exercises using a plastic device called a Triflow.

As instructed, I took strong, prolonged inhalations, causing a marker to rise to a target level. I was supposed to do these breathing exercises several times an hour. Not an easy task, and it was boring. However, I didn't want the staff to think I was a slacker, so I listened carefully for the nurse's footsteps as she approached my room to check on me. Just before she reached my door, I quickly picked up the Triflow, started breathing into it and counting aloud my repetitions: (breathe) ... "98" ... (breathe) ... "99" ... (breathe) ..."100."

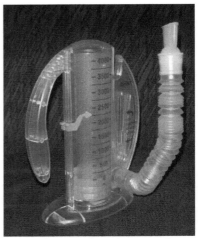

After three days of this, I needed to jazz it up a bit, so I took the Kazoo I brought from home—which I kept handy to entertain guests—and inserted it into the breathing hose of the Triflow. From then on, I not only breathed into the device, but hummed my favorite tunes at the same time.

I was released from the hospital on the fifth day. Sedated by pain medication, I clutched a pillow to my abdomen as I slept on the two-hour drive from San Francisco to our home in the Central Valley. I dreamt of the time to come I'd be well enough to get out and about. I was on a mission.

But first, I had to spend another month in a rented hospital bed.

TIP #27:

Trust God. He knows what it'll take to get the job done. "And we know that in all things God works for the good of those who love Him, who have been called according to His purpose" (Romans 8:28).

TIP #28:

Hospital patient pack list. Be sure to take your toothbrush, slippers, robe and disco ball earrings.

TIP #29:

Six inch photo button. If given the opportunity to have a picture button of yourself made, go for it. It may come in handy one day.

Chapter Sixteen
TAKING IT TO THE STREETS

Been There — Got The Wig!® ministry began as a one-woman campaign to educate women about the symptoms and treatment of ovarian cancer. Only four months after my second-look surgery, I came out swinging as I took to the streets of downtown to warn women about ovarian cancer.

(The Record, CA, October 9, 2007)

My hair grew in curly, temporarily, and was now more salt than pepper. I wore red scrubs to represent the blood of over 25 thousand women nationwide who are diagnosed each year; and the 16 thousand women who will lose their lives to the deadliest of the gynecologic cancers.

I wanted to tell women there is no screening test for ovarian cancer, nor is it detected by their annual Pap test. And according to the Ovarian Cancer National Alliance, "Until there's a test, Awareness is best." Women should know the symptoms, what to do if cancer is suspected, and where to go for more information.

I held this sign as an attention-getter, and introduced myself to women I met standing on the street. Some women passed by me awkwardly, unwilling to stop and listen to words that may save their lives. One lady quipped, "I'm a nurse, I know about ovarian cancer," as she dodged me on the side walk. All I could do was hope she wouldn't be that one woman out of fifty-seven to get it.

Several women said they thought routine Pap smears tested for ovarian cancer. They do not. Pap smears only test for cervical cancer.

The vague symptoms that whisper ovarian cancer commonly go unheard and misdiagnosed, and are usually discovered in latter stages beyond a cure. However, with early detection and proper treatment, survival rates increase to over ninety percent.

I urged women to get the facts about ovarian cancer from the Ovarian Cancer National Alliance. I prompted them to see a healthcare professional if symptoms are unusual for them, and persist.

I shared what they should look for: abdominal pressure, bloating, or discomfort; nausea, indigestion, or gas; constipation, diarrhea, or frequent urination; abnormal bleeding; unusual fatigue; unexplained weight loss or gain; shortness of breath.

According to the OCNA, all women are at risk for ovarian cancer, but some are at higher risk. Women who get ovarian cancer often have a family or personal history of ovarian, breast or colon cancer; not bearing children; increasing age.

Ovarian cancer risk may be reduced by taking oral contraceptives; pregnancy and breast-feeding; tubal ligation/hysterectomy; removal of the ovaries.

Until a screening test is found, it is recommended that women: have an annual vaginal/rectal pelvic exam. Women who are at high risk should discuss regular monitoring with their doctor. If she experiences symptoms, she should ask for a trans-vaginal ultrasound and a CA125 blood test.

Most importantly, if ovarian cancer is suspected, women should immediately consult a Gynecologic Oncologist. To find one in her area, she can call the Gynecologic Cancer Foundation at 1.800.444.4441.

For more information: Ovarian Cancer National Alliance, 901 E Street N.W. Suite 405, Washington, DC 20004, ocna@ovariancancer.org 202.331.1332. Toll free 1.866.3996262. Fax 202.331.2292, www.ovariancancer.org

For me, the best part of this street ministry was some women did listen to my warning. And if I saved just one woman, it was worth any self-consciousness I felt as I stood on the corner wearing red scrubs and holding a sign.

TAKING IT BACK TO THE DOCTORS

It took me nearly a year to build up the courage to go back to the doctors who repeatedly misdiagnosed me, and confront them. Again, I didn't blame the doctors for not recognizing the symptoms of ovarian cancer, because they are not cancer specialists trained to do so.

It was not their inability to identify the cause that was my problem. What I was angry about was they did not refer me to a specialist when they were apparently stumped. Their hesitation to do so could have shortened my life.

I wanted them to know I believed they blew it by failing to hear me when I insisted there was "something pressing inside me." In retrospect, I thought they should have responded to my description by including a CT scan and/or ultrasound, which would have revealed the tumors sooner and hastened my treatment. I maintained they should have eliminated the life-threatening possibilities like cancer first, then work the "pulled muscle in the gym" theory.

But most importantly, I wanted to make my doctors aware of the ovarian cancer symptoms which whisper, in the hope this knowledge may help them save other women's lives by early diagnosis and specialist referral.

Because I detest confrontations, it took a long time to get up my nerve to see my doctors face to face. I also thought it was a good idea to wait until my displaced anger had dissipated a bit. When I felt ready, I would start with the first ob-gyn doctor who missed the mark, and go prayed up.

I called the doctor's office and made an appointment to speak with her. I told the receptionist, "Do not charge me for this appointment. I will not pay to come in to give the doctor information she will want to know. I have finally identified my mystery disorder."

SURPRISE!

"So what was it?" the doctor asked as she entered the small exam room. I stood up, lifted my T-shirt, unzipped my jeans and dropped them low to reveal the full length of my surgical scar, took off my wig to show my bald head, and replied, "Ovarian cancer."

That was what is known as a Kodak moment. Her eyes bugged out, her mouth dropped open and stayed open for several moments while I filled in the details. I will never forget the shocked look on that doctor's face. I'd have snapped a picture of her reaction if my hands weren't busy holding up my pants and clutching my wig.

I gave her the information cards from the Ovarian Cancer National Alliance, which included symptoms and where to go for help, and asked her to make them available to other patients by displaying them in the waiting room. She vowed she would do so, and thanked me. I never went back to her again.

UNCOMFORTABLE

It was tougher for me to confront my general practitioner, because he was the doctor who I thought shined me on each time I specifically requested an ultrasound. This was the doctor who gave me a cortisone shot with an eight inch needle, albeit unknowingly, right into the tumor.

As I started to speak to him, he looked down at my medical file and continued to turn the pages. My heart was pounding as I told him I wanted him to look me in the eye when I say what I came to say. He complied.

"It's not your fault you missed the cancer, because you are not a cancer specialist. Other doctors missed it as well." I was surprised I didn't tell him off, because I certainly had considered it. Maybe I was growing. Or more likely, the Lord answered my prayer and gave me the words to speak. Besides, it wouldn't have served any purpose at that point.

I did tell him I was angry with him for not listening to me during four office visits when I repeatedly asked for an ultrasound. While I waited for his response, I thought, *It would be nice if he apologized to me.* I wanted him to apologize, but he didn't.

"So, are you cured now?" was all he said. I replied, "I'll tell you what the cancer doctor told me, and then I'll tell you why I don't fit the prognosis. According to the gynecologic oncologist, the two operations and six months of chemotherapy did not cure me, only bought me some time. But I believe the Lord has healed me by Jesus' stripes." Silence.

A POSITIVE SPIN

I continued, "It may be too late for me, but I'm here today to ask you to help me save other women who will wait in these exam rooms. I have created these bright yellow 8x10 laminated cards, which include the symptoms of ovarian cancer and where to go to follow up.

If there had been such a poster about ovarian cancer taped to the wall, I would have read it while I waited for you; and when you came into my room, I could have alerted you I had all six of the symptoms. I would like to see one of these cards posted in every room. Let's work together to save more women."

To the doctor's credit he posted the laminated warning cards in every exam room, and even in the waiting area in the lobby.

Praise God.

TIP #30:

Go prayed up. When confronting those whom you believe hurt or disappointed you, discard emotive or accusatory language, talk the facts, speak from the heart, smile if you can. Most importantly, prepare in prayer. "Lord, put one hand on my shoulder and your other hand across my mouth. Let me speak only words which will honor you."

TIP #31:

P.S.   " ... and please send in a few of your angels for backup. The really big and tall ones."

Chapter Seventeen
Been There — Got The Wig!® Breakfast Club

There's hope in knowing you're not alone. That's the reason I founded the Been There — Got The Wig!® Breakfast Club, a group for women Chemo Buddies who are currently undergoing, or about to start, treatment for any type of cancer, who meet for comradery, conversation and comfort food.

COMRADERY

Family and friends are limited in the support they can give, and soon they just want to return to normal life. We can empathize, because we have been there. We are women reaching out to other women in a difficult time in their lives. We share the same fear and the same hope.

The Breakfast Club provides positive, upbeat, faith-based support in a small group setting. I limit the number of women I invite per breakfast to no more than four, including myself, in order to create and maintain an intimate, personal environment. That's also the number of people who fit comfortably at a table in the restaurant.

There is no regularly set day or time for our meetings. The dates vary depending upon who and how many feel up to coming. Buy-Your-Own breakfast is the routine. Separate checks keeps it simple, and eliminates the testing of my math skills to divide the bill.

The Breakfast Club motto is, "A cheerful heart is good medicine" (Proverbs 17:22). We celebrate milestones, like counting down to the end of chemo treatments, or getting a new wig, CT scans, or the long-awaited re-growth of hair. We thank God for every day. We celebrate life ... and breakfast.

CONVERSATION

The first thing I always tell women beginning this journey is to call and sign up with the American Cancer Society. The ACS provides many free services for cancer patients, such as travel to and from treatment, Look Good ... Feel Better class, hats and scarves, etc., and a mountain of valuable resource materials.

While we don't give medical advice, we do share information we have gleaned through our individual experiences. One of my goals has been to encourage women to get second and third opinions at different medical centers specializing in their type of cancer. And to always check with their oncologist when they have any questions regarding symptoms or treatment.

If the ladies are considering getting a wig, I refer or accompany them to Bobbie Stoller at The Wig Palace, (209) 339-4083. Bobbie taught me the time to choose a wig is before they lose their hair to chemo, so they can best match their own color and style. When we look better, we feel better.

We laugh a lot too. One morning a gal said since going through chemo, her body just wasn't the same. SENSITIVE SUBJECT ALERT: She added, when she peed, it ran down her thigh because "her shooter is now crooked." Oddly enough, I was able to offer an explanation to this phenomenon, as I too spent months peeing down my thighs every time I went to the bathroom.

What I learned: Pubic hair directs the urine away from the body, and then gravity takes over and the stream flows down into the toilet. Without pubic hair, the urine exits through the urethra and then follows the line of the body. This was especially annoying when I'd go in a public restroom, because I had to plan ahead, and take a wet paper towel with me into the stall in order to swab my thighs after peeing. Who knew pubic hair had a practical function?

COMFORT FOOD

The best breakfast in town is at Avenue Grill. Really, Avenue Grill was voted "Best Breakfast in Town," largely in part to the smiling owner/chef, Mike Metcalf, who is usually found standing behind the counter, cooking. His personal touch is also added to the food offerings, such as French Toast, "Made the way my mom did."

Disclaimer: One day

he confessed to me the French toast isn't really made the way his mom did. His candid admission caused me to wonder about the pancakes.

The hot cakes are called giant flapjacks, and they are:

The blueberry hot cake pictured here is the small version, and it still covers the edge of a 10-inch dinner plate.

I've observed Mike always errs on the side of "give them more." It's not uncommon for him to add an extra piece of bacon or egg to the order, just because. I also recently discovered if I order my one egg scrambled instead of fried, I get the equivalent of at least two eggs, because he uses a big ladle to pour the egg mixture onto the grill rather than cracking one egg.

In addition to breakfast served all day, Mike's menu includes a variety of great hamburgers, sandwiches and salads. The large portions are matched by the friendliness and efficiency of his staff. Most importantly, Avenue Grill has been a warm and welcoming home for the Been There – Got The Wig!® Breakfast Club.

HOPE IS CONTAGIOUS

I've learned the best way to fight this cancer battle is to reach out to others who are going through the same experience, and encourage them. I recently found this card from my friend Rosie. It touched me then and now.

Jana: I thank God for Allowing our paths to cross in our Journey to the "Promise Land". you ████ a real blessing to my life. I really admire your strength & Courage! My journey has been easier because of you, even when your down you always encourage me. Our friendship is special to me! "I thank God for you" I just wanted you to know / I really enjoyed our Day in Sacramento, Can't wait til we do another Fun Day Again
Lots of prayers & Love

Rosie
2007

P.S. I was writing while on Chemo as you can see HA! HA!

So as you continue this journey,
I'll continue to ask the Lord
to give you peace, hope,
and everything you need
for every step you take.
He is the one who knows you best—
heart, soul, and body—
and He will take care of you.

Hope you feel better real Soon! "Lots of Rest IS Best"! !

REMEMBERING ROSIE

Rosie and I were the two original 'chemo buddies,' as we called ourselves, and she the charter member of my Been There — Got The Wig!® Breakfast Club. Rosie and I became close friends, but we didn't start out that way.

Although we attended the same church and knew of each other, we were not drawn to each other as friends. We seemed to be so different from one another. Little did we know we would soon become sisters as we fought a common battle.

She was diagnosed with breast cancer at the same time I found out I had ovarian cancer. Our mutual friend, JoAnn Lee, told me, "HEY, YOU SHOULD CALL ROSIE AND YOU TWO GALS GET TOGETHER, BECAUSE YOU'RE BOTH GOING THROUGH THE SAME THING!" (JoAnn's enthusiasm translates to all CAPS and an exclamation mark in printed form.)

We called, met for breakfast, and shared our feelings and responses to our varied treatments. We never asked, God, "Why me, why her?"

But together we answered ... "Why not us?" God knew we would speak up and reach out to other women who face this battle. We would empathize, because we walk in the same shoes.

I remember one breakfast when a woman who was newly diagnosed with cancer and beside herself with fright, asked, "How do you find the faith to get through this?" And without hesitation, Rosie looked her in the eye and said, "I have the faith because I have Jesus Christ living in my heart, and I know He is in charge of my life." Rosie continued, explaining it's possible to "have peace as we walk through this cancer experience because Jesus is with us."

On several occasions, I watched and listened to Rosie witness to the ladies who joined our intimate little group. I was impressed she spoke with such confidence, authority, and yet gentleness. We were a good team. I brought them in, and Rosie was the closer.

Rosie and I often reflected on the fact we would never have pegged us to be such close friends, because we are so different from one another; but through this journey we discovered we shared the same heart.

We laughed too. I'll never forget the time when we went to Mimi's for breakfast, and as we walked into the crowded restaurant, I told Rosie the pain medication I took after my second operation caused significant hearing loss. I added I could not gauge the volume of my voice, and asked her to give me a signal if I was talking too loud.

I just couldn't resist. As she studied the menu, I deliberately shouted out, "WHAT ARE YOU GOING TO ORDER?!" Rosie never looked up from her menu, but her eyes got as big as saucers ... and she forgot to give me the signal.

Rosie was a hero. Not just because she fought cancer for over four years, but because throughout her fight she continued to trust God, to praise God, and to encourage others to do the same. She showed great strength and courage. Rosie met fear with faith.

Rosie was the catalyst and, in part, inspiration for my Been There— Got the Wig!® Breakfast Club & Ministry. She went to be with the Lord in March, 2011. She was always in my corner, and she will live in my heart forever.

TIP #32:

Hang out with positive people. Hope is contagious.

TIP #33:

Help others who are going through similar circumstances. There's healing in knowing you're not alone.

Chapter Eighteen
FIGHTING BACK BY GIVING BACK

Just as there's hope in knowing you're not alone, there's strength in having others in your corner as you fight against cancer. A good place to start is to join forces with the American Cancer Society, which raises funds for research, education and treatment, and provides a multitude of services to cancer patients.

The ACS signature fund raiser is Relay For Life. "Teams of people camp out at a local high school, park, or fairground, and take turns walking or running around a track or path. Each team has a representative on the track at all times during the event. Because cancer doesn't sleep, Relays are overnight events up to twenty-four hours in length."

The Relay For Life motto is Celebrate, Remember, Fight Back. Survivors are celebrated in The Survivors Lap, as they circle the track together.

Relay For Life, 2009

Chemo Buddy Wilma

People who have been touched by cancer and loved ones who have lost their fight, are honored in The Luminaria Ceremony after dark.

We are Survivors

Chemo buddy Kathy, wind & rain

We left Relay and drove to Avenue Grill for breakfast and to show off our Survivor medals.

The next day in the News-Sentinel ...

The Fight Back Ceremony includes "making a personal commitment to save lives by taking up the fight against cancer. That commitment may be as simple as talking to elected officials about cancer or getting a screening test. By taking action, people are personally taking steps to save lives and fight back against a disease that takes too much."

IT IS WHAT IT IS

I've known friends who lost their fight with cancer before it began, because they didn't want to know what was wrong with them, as though not knowing would keep the disease at bay. The problem with the denial approach is they already had it, whatever it was. So why not find out its name and how to fight it.

The first weapon against cancer is early detection. We've all heard that message. The people who win this battle are the ones who come out of the doctor's office swinging, and don't give up. NEVER, NEVER, GIVE UP!!

SPEAKING FROM EXPERIENCE

It was my honor to be the guest Survivor Speaker at the Opening Ceremony for the 2011 Relay For Life in Stockton, California.

After speaking, I enjoyed walking around the grounds and meeting other Survivors as I stopped at booths set up by the relay teams. In addition to collecting pledge money, several of the teams raised extra funds by offering various items for raffle.

I didn't bother to sign up for free drawings because I never win. And because I already had the prize I wanted, my restored health. I wasn't in the least bit tempted to play the game of chance.

Not even when I came upon the plum, the treasure, the humdinger, the big catch of the day. I'm talkin' the cherry ... a woman's 26" pink and white Schwinn bicycle. That prize was the buzz of the Relay. The large jar filled with raffle tickets of hopeful Relay goers reflected that the odds of winning the bike were fat chance.

Earlier in the day my friend told me she desperately desired the pink Schwinn. With longing in her voice and body language to match, she declared, "I want that bike!"

Without telling my friend, I snuck back to the booth alone and bought one five-dollar ticket. I didn't think there was any point of buying three tickets for ten-dollars because I never win.

As I paid my money and wrote my name on the raffle ticket, I prayed: "Lord, my friend really wants this bike. If you'll give me the bike, I'll give it to her and I'll be sure to tell her it is from you."

Given my non-winning history with giveaway drawings, I went home at the end of the day and promptly forgot about it. Later that night I got a phone call from the Relay Team leader excitedly informing me I had won the pink bike!

It was all I could do to resist calling my friend to give her the news, but I resisted. This surprise warranted a face-to-face reveal. I waited until Monday, then loaded the bike into the van and drove to her office. I told her I was running errands in the neighborhood and stopped by to say "Hi." So that it wasn't a lie, I shopped at a couple stores on my way home.

Anyway, I asked her to accompany me out to the parking lot to see what my husband was carrying in his car. Before lifting the back door I told her I had a God story to tell her. She said, "Oh good. I like those stories."

A KODAK MOMENT

As I opened the door I announced, "I won your bike." I don't know which one of us was more thrilled. She teared up and her mouth remained open as I climbed into the van. While we unloaded the bike I told her the story behind this remarkable turn of events. That God is not a genie or a Santa Claus; that He knows us, knows the number of hairs on our heads; that He knows the desires of our hearts; and what I prayed as I filled out the raffle ticket.

I told her, "After this, you don't ever have to question if God is real. If He knows you. If He knows what you're going through. The Lord gave you the desire of your heart, this bike, so you would know He is with you, and He's aware of what you want as well as what you need. And from now on, no matter what happens to you in life or whatever challenge you face, you will know He is there."

A TWO-FER

My friend got the bike and I got the answer to my prayer. We were both touched, and now we share a God story to remember.

TIP #34:

There's strength in numbers. Reaching out to others can take the focus off your pain, your heartache.

TIP #35:

"Delight yourself in the Lord and He will give you the desires of your heart." (Psalm 37:4)

Chapter Nineteen
I SURPRISED MY DOCTORS

I lived to celebrate a milestone birthday.

As a cancer survivor, now every birthday is a milestone to be celebrated. Even the half year counts. I'm looking forward to seventy with renewed enthusiasm.

I SEE THE FUTURE

The Good News was I was still alive. The Bad News was I was getting older and my eyesight was continuing to worsen with age. I was dependent upon trifocals to see near and far and in between. When my eye doctor told me I was a candidate for Laser Vision Correction, I got excited about seeing my future more clearly.

I had heard the procedure is quick, painless, and affords immediate vision improvement. I'd also heard that if you move or blink during the operation, you'd be permanently blind. No pressure.

The staff was confident of success, and noticeably enthusiastic. I wondered why they were so happy. The ambience was unusually celebratory for a medical office.

The first step was to relax my pre-op nerves with a little Valium.

I wasn't sure the drug was working.

Then off to the operating room.

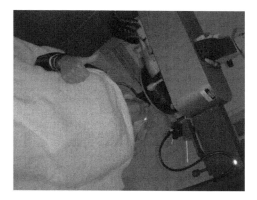

After the procedure, a commemorative photo with the doctor.

I could see the clock on the wall for the first time in years! Then I understood why the staff was so joyful. They knew they were in the miracle business.

TIP #36:

"We live by faith, not by sight" (2 Corinthians 5:7) But if you need your vision laser corrected, just do it. Life's too short to not see the leaves on the trees, or the clock on the wall, etc.

Chapter Twenty

OUT OF MY COMFORT ZONE & EMBRACING LIFE

Before cancer, if I saw a stranger holding a sign that read "Free Hugs," I would have been amused at the idea, and maybe just for an instant, considered it. In the end, I'd have crossed the street to avoid the offer, while secretly wishing I had the confidence and nerve to receive a free hug.

Well, on a trip to New York I was faced with that choice. My teenage son and I were walking around Times Square when I spotted the Free Hugs people in the middle of the street.

I wanted to break out of my shell and be more of a participant in life, still I hesitated and contemplated walking away. But then I asked myself, *"If not now—when?"* So I ran to get my hug from a stranger.

While we were hugging, she informed me, "Now you have to hold the sign until someone comes and hugs you."

I panicked inside. *I could refuse to do it, put the sign down, and walk away.*

But I didn't!

I stood in the middle of Times Square holding a Free Hugs sign! Which, by the way, totally mortified my teenage son who stayed back on the curb and took the picture.

Holding this sign was like waiting to be picked for the basketball team in junior high P.E. class. As I watched people approach other sign holders, I hoped and prayed I wouldn't have long to wait. Then I heard a gleeful scream, and turned to see a tall woman running towards me to get her hug.

After passing the sign on to her, I followed my son, who by that time was pretending he didn't know me, as he continued walking up the street.

GOD'S LOVE — LIFE'S FREE HUG

I think God's love is a little like a free hug in that some people run with their arms stretched out to receive it, and others walk away. It does seem too good to be true ... God created and maintains the universe, and yet knows the number of hairs on our heads, calls us friend, is concerned about our struggles, knows what we want, but gives us what we need.

For example, my mom and I celebrated every one of my birthdays together until I was in my 50s and Alzheimer's disease had stolen our tradition. Despite other affirmations, I just did not feel birthdayed until the two of us lunched, laughed, shopped, and I spent the one hundred dollars she usually gave me.

So when Mom forgot my birthday for the first time in my life, it signaled the slipping away of our special mother/daughter relationship. I grieved as I struggled with whether or not to tell her she'd forgotten my birthday. Because of our unique life bond I thought she would want to know, and re-schedule our celebration.

Yet, I was afraid she would become distressed at the evidence she was losing her mind. I did not want to take the chance of hurting her, but I desired to hang onto our tradition, our life together, a little longer. And then there was the ...

I confess I also wanted my birthday money. I prayed for wisdom.

ANSWERED PRAYER

I bought gum at Walmart and was about to exit through the double doors when the cashier came running after me and excitedly said, "Ma'am you dropped this." She held out her hand and opened it to reveal a one hundred dollar bill folded into a small square. I told her, "It's not mine," and kept walking.

She insisted it was, "I saw this fall out of your purse." Again I calmly said, "It's not mine," and shrugged my shoulder to punctuate my claim. She remained unconvinced to believe my denial rather than her own eyes.

By then a small crowd had gathered around us at the store entrance. More than one customer offered to take the money. As I turned and walked out the door, I heard the clerk exclaim, "You've got to be kidding me!"

I guess she was surprised I wouldn't take the money and run. But I knew it wasn't mine, and to accept it would have been stealing.

As I walked through the parking lot to my car, I heard the Lord say to me, "I can give you one hundred dollars anytime I want. You don't need your mother's money."

That was a day I'll never forget. I bet the store clerk won't ever forget it either, but for a different reason.

I did not tell Mom she missed my birthday. It would have served no purpose. And as it turned out, I received so much more than a passing birthday celebration. I got the thrill of God speaking to me and affirming He does know what I want; and the gratification of Him giving me what I needed, an answer to a daughter's prayer.

TIP #37:

Step off the curb, and out of your comfort zone. Do something you've always wanted to do, as long as it is moral and legal, that is. Embrace life.

TIP #38:

Ask God for what you want. Trust Him to give you what you need.

TIP #39:

Go for the free hug.

Chapter Twenty-One
THE GIFT OF CANCER ... WHAT?

As it turned out, cancer was a gift. Through this experience I was forever changed for the better, in mind and spirit. My faith deepened, appreciation for life magnified, attitude adjusted, time management improved, horizon broadened, future focused. These are all gifts that played a role in the reinvention of me after cancer.

FAITH

Cancer gave me the gift of a closer walk with the Lord. Throughout my battle with cancer, I felt God's love for me as He gave me the strength and courage I needed to endure two operations and chemotherapy. As I recuperated, He gave me the reassurance I needed He hadn't forgotten me. And today, God gives me the faith I need to not live in fear of cancer coming back.

Cancer allowed me to experience how God gives us the tools we need to go through and overcome a difficult circumstance or hardship. I found hope in Christ; and the Lord turned my mourning into dancing and my sorrow into joy.

LIFE'S TOO SHORT

I learned life truly is too short to spend time with negative people; to not wear my good clothes everyday; or to not order dessert whenever I want.

And I stopped acquiring lots of stuff for the house. My life is no longer defined by material possessions, a fabulous wardrobe excluded. I still want to look great.

A NEW REFERENCE POINT

Since cancer, I've adopted a different way of measuring the severity of the challenges I face in life. When trouble comes, I testify, "The situation is bad, but it's not cancer." This assertion is a simple reminder things could be a lot worse, so don't sweat the small stuff.

I LEARNED A LOT

Another thing I learned was not to put things off. I am not ordinarily a procrastinator, but I had been paying for a web domain for over a year without starting construction on the site. My perceived obstacle to beginning the project, and subsequent hesitation, was that it would involve technology. And because I didn't know what I was doing in that arena, I did nothing.

After cancer, I followed through with the designing and publishing of my own website. I used one of those make-your-own-site builders, which walked me through the step-by-step process.

The first step was to choose a background color and design template. Now that took me a while because I had to look at each of the two thousand backgrounds before making my choice. I wondered *what if the next template was even better than the last?* The final selection was a no-brainer, for there was only one background in my favorite, signature colors: red, black, white.

I painstakingly created the multi-page site, including font choice, writing copy, uploading pictures, my YouTube video clips, and radio interviews. Days later the new website was completed. I was so excited! I was finally going to have an official website!

Oh what a proud and happy day it was, for I had jumped in with both feet and I had overcome my trepidation of modern technology. I held my breath as I clicked the mouse to publish the site to the web.

Next, I Googled www.janaflaig.com to see what the world would see. To my horror I saw I had inadvertently published the site builder Sample Page along with my pages.

Instead of Speaker/Humorist, the bio on the Sample Page said I was an Actress/Model. At first I couldn't figure out if I had done something wrong, or if the site builder company was trying to guess my occupation. To make matters worse, my age from some other internet source—public records or maybe a newspaper article about the Been There—Got The Wig!® Breakfast Club—was somehow included.

Luckily, I was able to delete the erroneous Sample Page, but I could not delete or change the website heading which continued to appear on the Google index page. I was still listed as Jana Flaig, Middle-Aged Female, Actress/Model, which everyone knows is code for a Cougar Escort Service.

As a middle-aged female I was humiliated. I didn't get a single call.

A GOAL COMPLETED

Despite a few glitches, I was thrilled to have launched my own website. And if I say so myself, it quickly became popular in cyberspace. In just the first day of being published, the site got ninety hits!

Well, actually, one hit was from the site builder company thanking me for my business, one hit from Jean Danna, my girl-friend in Georgia, and the other eighty-eight hits were from me. I kept checking to see if it was still there.

I WENT FOR IT

Before cancer, I could be spontaneous only if it was well planned in advance. After cancer, I've loosened up a bit. For example, at the private high school fundraiser, I quickly got into the spirit of the event by bidding on the first auction item, Principal for a Day. Admittedly, I was prompted by the description in the program: "How would you like to be in charge? As long as it is moral and legal, YOU call the shots."

Going once ... going twice ... SOLD!

Value: PRICELESS

I implemented my "Open Door" policy.

How hard can this job be, anyway?

Directing the morning car line was my first order of business.

I kept traffic moving smoothly and connected with parents.

"No, I'm not qualified for the principal's job."

"I'm more of an example of The Peter Principle for a Day."

I interacted with students in the classroom.

I shared how I squeezed four years of college into ten.

I interrupted classes to give live announcements over the P.A. system. Announcement #1:

"In-N-Out's coming to us for lunch. I've called a special assembly this afternoon, including The Eddie Haskell Kiss Up Awards. F.Y.I., you'll find a Tip Jar on the counter in the office."

Announcement #2:

"You may spend five minutes of class time texting. And I thank the student who put a Monster drink in the Tip Jar.

IfeellikeI'mtalkingveryfast,butIcan'treallytell."

Lunch time:

It can be lonely at the top.

At the assembly.

"I thank the principal and staff for their welcoming attitude, and apologize for the small fire in the school office."

"And I don't know how the secretary got locked in the supply closet for seven hours."

"Doctors say she'll recover, and begin to speak again in a couple of weeks."

I declared Friday a free dress day. The teachers were given a choice between detention or dancing for the students. And to my surprise ...

... they chose to participate in a choreographed dance number, Michael Jackson's *Thriller*. Which proves that even teachers will do anything to avoid detention."

Finally ... 2:30 P.M.

How does the principal do it? Next time I'll bid on the 18-pound box of cherries.

TIP #40:

<u>Don't be out bid in life</u>. Go for it. And be sure to take lots of pictures.

TIP #41:

<u>Look for the gift in your hardship</u>. "... suffering produces perseverance; perseverance, character; and character, hope. And hope does not disappoint us, because God has poured out His love into our hearts by the Holy Spirit, whom He has given us" (Romans 5:3-5).

Chapter Twenty-Two
FINDING THE FUNNY

Cancer isn't funny. Nor are various hardships such as divorce, job loss, death of a loved one, foreclosure, illness, or other difficult circumstances. As I've said, things were going good for me before cancer. My life was like a Christmas stocking filled with wonderful gifts. When I was diagnosed, it was as though someone put a four-ton elephant of fear in my stocking, which overwhelmed me, robbed me of hope, decreased my faith, and threatened to defeat me.

The greatest challenge I faced in this battle was taming that elephant, rendering fear docile and powerless over me. I succeeded with humor, positive attitude and, most significantly, by reaching out to the Lord. As a result, today I possess a stronger faith, and a deeper relationship with God. I am an over-comer.

No, cancer isn't funny, but I've learned it's possible to find humor in the process of going through a difficult circumstance.

I'm not sure whether humor and laughter created my positive attitude, or if the reverse allowed me to find the funny in my fight against cancer. Either way, like it says in Proverbs 17:22, "a cheerful heart" was "good medicine" for me.

LAUGHTER, LIFE'S MEDICINE

Medical studies have proven this is true. It is reported laughter releases endorphins, activates the immune system, and decreases stress hormones. So, laughter can lift our spirits. I can vouch for that. I found when I laughed I felt better, and when I felt better, it was easier to hang on to hope. And if there's one thing I needed most, it was hope. With hope came courage, and with courage came strength. "But those who hope in the Lord will renew their strength. They will soar on wings like eagles; they will run and not be weary; they will walk and not be faint" (Isaiah 40:31).

Drinking in the comedy of life helped me recognize humor in my own struggles. I believe finding that humor throughout my cancer treatments allowed me to regain some sense of control, which I'd lost when the doctor told me I had The BIG C. Cancer, with all its pain, discomfort, disfiguration, fear and hair loss, equaled total lack of control. It was polar to my "I'VE DECIDED TO PUT MYSELF IN CHARGE" campaign.

Laughter was and is an integral part of my survivorship. I thank God I was born with a sense of humor, that it was further developed by my mother, and sharpened through this cancer odyssey.

"A DAY WITHOUT LAUGHTER IS A DAY WASTED"

Today I continue to watch funny videos, TV shows and movies. I get a big laugh out of the many clips on YouTube, especially the ones in which animals act like people. When I'm driving in my car I listen to an All Comedy radio station.

One of my favorite past times is to spend time in a toy store, where I find many light-hearted and fun things, like a sliding bird whistle, or a sound machine with canned laughter. But mostly, I try to hang out with people who make me laugh.

Humor and laughter have always played an important role in my life. Perhaps without realizing it, I've been trained to look at life through humor glasses. I grew up watching and imitating, studying really, Lucille Ball, Red Skelton, Jerry Lewis, Carol Burnett and others on television. Doing so didn't make me funnier, it enhanced my perception of the funny that happens around us everyday.

IT ALL STARTED ...

... when I was a preschooler in an era when kids were more isolated, as they stayed home until age five before entering Kindergarten. I looked forward to the parties my parents hosted, because I was allowed to greet their guests before I went to bed.

One night I was very excited to share with them a milestone in my short life. Earlier that day I had learned how to spell my first word. After making that brief announcement, the adults congratulated me and urged me to demonstrate my newly acquired knowledge. In that moment I envisioned my future dotted with spelling bees.

The room was silent and all eyes were on me as I drew in a big breath. Slowly I enunciated each of the letters to spell my inaugural word: "B"... "M." The response was instantaneous and unexpected. The grownups burst into laughter, and my mother quickly announced, "Okay, bedtime," as she scooped me up and carried me horizontally under her arm to my room. As I laid in my bed wondering what just happened, I could still hear the laughter bouncing off the walls in the living room. I was hooked.

IN CONCLUSION, A TIP

I offer a little safety trick I learned which aided me in walking with a walker in the hospitals so soon after my major surgeries. When I had to get myself up out of bed in the middle of the night to go to the toilet, the room beyond my area light was dark, making the walk all the way from my bed to the restroom potentially hazardous.

I tried using a small night light which I brought from home and plugged into the wall, but it only illuminated the space around my bed, not the distance to the restroom.

Next, I tried carrying a lantern which I

could take with me as I slowly shuffled across the floor, but I quickly realized I needed both hands free to hold on to the walker. So the lantern was not the answer either.

I finally came up with a solution that lighted my path and allowed me to walk with my hands on the walker ...

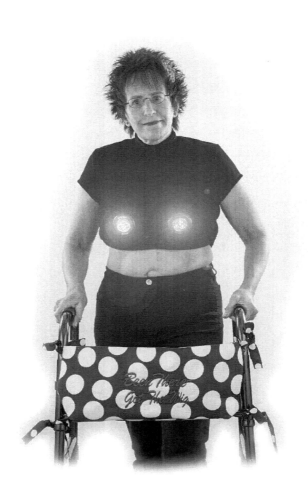

I bought these lights on sale. They were buy one, get one free.

And with that BIG cut and all those staples, I was bent over, so the lights were pointing the right way ...

Now this is a very practical tip you can use. And if you're a full-figured gal, I know what you're thinking ...

... but I got you covered.

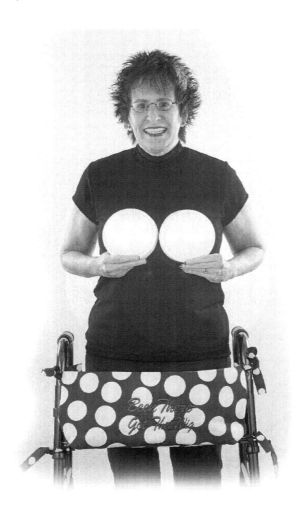

TIP #42:

Add humor. Watch funny movies or television shows each day. Read a joke book. Listen to the All Comedy station on satellite radio.

TIP #43:

Hang out with people who make you laugh.

Chapter Twenty-Three
FIGHT FEAR AND FOSTER FAITH

No matter what the difficult circumstance or hardship, with it often comes fear. With fear comes doubt, and together they impair or weaken faith. Fear is the reverse of faith.

We need not be defeated by fear as we walk through life's valleys if we go through them with the Lord. When we knock out fear along the way, we strengthen our faith, and by our faith God gives us the tools we need to endure every step.

"There is no fear in love. But perfect love drives out fear" (1 John 4:18). Ultimately it is God's love for us, and our relationship with Him that brings the hope and courage we need to overcome.

We may go ten rounds before we learn the tips to knock out fear; but once we do that, we are free to take our lives off pause and move forward. Living without fear makes us champs. Put on your boxing gloves and fight fear!

TIPS IN REVIEW:

1. <u>Never let them see you sweat</u>. Being courageous doesn't mean we have no fear. Courage is persevering in spite of fear.

2. <u>Request the 1960's version</u> of the anesthesiologist's happy juice if you're ever in the hospital for major surgery.

3. <u>Wear your good clothes everyday</u>. Don't save them for a special occasion, or for someday when you'll be well again or life returns to normal. When you look better, you feel better. When you feel better, it's easier to have hope and to be encouraged.

4. Rethink the tattoo idea. I'm just saying.

5. Plan ahead. Teach your family members how to cook for themselves in case you're laid up and can't do it. Or at least show them, again, how to put the lid back onto the peanut butter jar.

6. Go to a specialist at one of the top teaching medical centers, such as UC San Francisco, UC Davis, or Stanford University, when faced with a serious health problem.

7. Be the squeaky wheel, whether the circumstance is career pursuits, health issues, relationships, etc.

8. Ask for help. Afford people the opportunity to be blessed by giving to you. That may include meals, household chores, praying together, encouraging cards, phone calls or visits.

9. Say "Yes" if a friend who's visiting asks, "Do you want me to vacuum the carpet or wash the dishes in the sink before I leave?"

10. Look for the postcards from God in your life. Do not return to sender unread.

11. Get at least a second opinion and get it from a specialist in the field.

12. Forgive people for the stupid things they say in their attempt to comfort you in your difficult circumstance. And ignore any comments that may feed fear.

13. Extinguish the fiery darts of the enemy by countering with God's Word. For example, (Philippians 4:13) "I can do everything through Him who gives me strength."

14. Watch your words. Positive speech promotes positive attitude, negative speech cultivates negative thinking. Pray victory, not defeat. "The tongue has the power of life and death" (Proverbs 18:21).

15. Run away from negative people. Even if they are blood related. I mean it.

16. Refuse to receive fear. Fear does not come from the Lord. "For God did not give us a spirit of timidity, but a spirit of power, of love, and of self-discipline" (2 Timothy 1:7). Rebuke fear in the

name of Jesus.

17. Don't go it alone. Tell friends, family, church leaders what you're going through so they can offer assistance. Seek support from other Christian believers. They are the ones who will stand in the gap for you, and lift you up in intercessory prayer.

18. Be the feisty one. Fight fear, don't surrender to it.

19. Reach out to God. Call upon Him and He will answer. "Do not fear, for I am with you; do not be dismayed, for I am your God. I will strengthen you and help you; I will uphold you with my righteous right hand" (Isaiah 41:10).

20. Hug your hair dresser. Just because.

21. Don't underestimate God. He is always one step ahead of us. Maybe more. He has a great memory, too.

22. Be careful what you pray for. Make your dream big enough for God to fit into, then step back.

23. Always have a Plan B. A little bit of preplanning can change a negative experience into a positive memory.

24. Always put on lipstick before walking to the mailbox. Mother was right.

25. Strength comes from the Lord. "Those who hope in the Lord will renew their strength" (Isaiah 40:31).

26. Never, never, never give up! Winston Churchill said, "When you're going through hell, keep going."

27. Trust God. He knows what it'll take to get the job done. "In all things God works for the good of those who love Him, who have been called according to His purpose" (Romans 8:28).

28. Hospital patient pack list. Be sure to take your toothbrush, slippers, robe and disco ball earrings.

29. Six inch photo button. If given the opportunity to have a picture button of yourself made, go for it. It may come in handy one day.

30. Go prayed up. When confronting those whom you believe hurt or disappointed you, discard emotive or accusatory language, talk the facts, speak from the heart, smile if you can. Most

importantly, prepare in prayer. "Lord, put one hand on my shoulder and your other hand across my mouth. Let me speak only words which will honor you."

31. P.S. " ... and please send in a few of your angels for backup. The ones that are really big and tall."

32. Hang out with positive people. Hope is contagious.

33. Help others who are going through a similar circumstance. There's healing in knowing I'm not alone.

34. There's strength in numbers. Reaching out to others can take the focus off your pain, your heartache.

35. "Delight yourself in the Lord and He will give you the desires of your heart" (Psalm 37:4).

36. "We live by faith, not by sight" (2 Corinthians 5:7). But if you need your vision laser corrected, just do it. Life's too short to not see the leaves on the trees, or the clock on the wall, etc.

37. Step off the curb, and out of your comfort zone. Do something you've always wanted to do, as long as it is moral and legal, that is. Embrace life.

38. Ask God for what you want. Trust Him to give you what you need.

39. Go for the free hug.

40. Don't be out bid in life. Go for it. And be sure to take lots of pictures.

41. Look for the gift in your hardship. " ... suffering produces perseverance; perseverance, character; character, hope. And hope does not disappoint us, because God has poured out His love into our hearts by the Holy Spirit, whom He has given us" (Romans 5:3-5).

42. Add humor. Watch funny movies or television shows each day. Read a joke book. Listen to the All Comedy Station on satellite radio.

43. Hang out with people who make you laugh.

ABOUT THE AUTHOR

JANA FLAIG, SPEAKER, INSPIRATIONAL HUMORIST, brings encouragement wrapped in humor.

She is a Professional Encourager who uplifts and engages her audiences with comedy, storytelling, demonstration and inventive visuals and props that create a fun, upbeat and memorable program. They call her "a hero—very courageous and wonderfully funny!"

Christian Comedy Association member since 2006, CCA is a networking community of Christian comedians and performers who support the use of comedy for outreach and promote clean entertainment. She showcased at CCA conference in 2011, 2012.

Two Released DVDs: *who put the elephant in my stocking?* and *Been There —Got The Wig!*®

Founder of the **BEEN THERE — GOT THE WIG!**® **Breakfast Club & Ministry**, a networking group of women "Chemo Buddies" who meet for comradery, conversation and comfort food. Endorsed by the American Cancer Society (regional branch, Stockton, CA), the club provides a positive, upbeat, faith-based environment for women currently undergoing or about to start treatment for any type of cancer.

Jana's a **Professional Speaker** (35 years), Special Events, Women's Conferences and Retreats, Seminar and Workshop Leader. As a member of National Speakers Association, she was featured speaker at the NSA Professional Speakers Educational Workshop, San Francisco, CA.

Former **TV News On-Air Reporter** and **Assignment Editor** in Los Angeles; **Associate Professor** of Broadcasting Arts and Speech Communication; **Media Trainer**.

M.A. Communications & Media, CSULB; **B.A.** Radio & Television, CSULB.

As a **cancer survivor**, Jana now wears her good clothes everyday, and orders dessert whenever she wants.

www.janaflaig.com